THE
HIDDEN
HISTORY
of the
MAIN
LINE

THE
HIDDEN
HISTORY
of the
MAIN
LINE

*From Philadelphia
to Malvern*

MARK E. DIXON

THE
History
PRESS

Published by The History Press
Charleston, SC 29403
www.historypress.net

First published 2010

Manufactured in the United States

ISBN 978.1.60949.064.5

Dixon, Mark E.
The hidden history of the Main Line : from Philadelphia to Malvern / Mark E. Dixon.
p. cm.
Includes bibliographical references.
ISBN 978-1-60949-064-5
1. Main Line (Pa.)--History. 2. Philadelphia Suburban Area (Pa.)--History. 3.
Pennsylvania--History, Local. 4. Main Line (Pa.)--Biography. 5. Philadelphia Suburban
Area (Pa.)--Biography. 6. Pennsylvania--Biography. I. Title.
F158.68.A1D59 2010
974.8'1--dc22
2010027744

Contents

CONTENTS

FOREWORD

From the beginning of America, writing "local" history has been the seedbed of nation-building. Early "American" writers such as Washington Irving, James Fenimore Cooper and Nathaniel Hawthorne, among others, drew on "local color" tales in finding their own American voice and creating an American literature, as well as folk tales, stories and sacred relics from local places that pointed Americans to their own histories devoid of Old World corruptions. At the same time, amateur scientists such as Benjamin Franklin, Thomas Jefferson and James Audubon, among others, recorded, gathered up and even transplanted native flora and fauna on their way to discovering and asserting an American natural history that seemed to promise a brave new world of abundance and possibility. In all this, then as now, locating and discovering one's own place among peoples and a continental expanse so diverse and vast as America has proved essential to any sense of rootedness. A people and a culture ever on the go need to be grounded in something more palpable and real than ideas imbedded in parchment promises such as the Declaration of Independence and the Constitution. They need connections to particular places and pasts to create any sense of community. Enter local history.

For a century or more from the beginning of the republic, local history writing was almost wholly the province of the "amateur," who collected the artifacts, tales and documents for display and description. The works they produced were antiquarian rather than analytical, but they were also unashamedly promotional in celebrating a past of progress and the virtues of a particular place and people. By the late nineteenth century, with the emergence of history as a profession ruled by new standards of "objectivity" and scientific method, local history writing moved, in part, into the hands of scholars supposedly taking a more critical assessment of the character and conduct of different people in different places, often within a comparative framework that showed both the uniqueness and sameness of American places. Local history also bloomed in the publication of numerous county histories that were encyclopedic in coverage and in illustrated histories gathering up postcards, photographs and other images to make "real" places and people no longer standing or alive. All the while, local historians published books, booklets and articles in magazines and newspapers that highlighted an event, building or personality worth remembering, often reverentially.

Local history writing gained new interest and a wider audience with the rise of the "new social history" from the 1960s on, in which historians shifted primacy from studying kings and queens to looking at the daily lives of the common sort and others. To do so, they found new purpose in the genealogical records, oral histories, folklore, architecture and anything left by people that revealed who they were, what they believed and why they behaved as they did. New interests invited new looks at the past, as women, immigrant and ethnic groups, minorities and others left out of the national narrative now entered the field of vision of local history and the "new social history." Then, too, the very mobility and instability of America, moving faster each decade, quickened interest in local history. Whether in an airline magazine, newspaper or any of the many local or regional magazines promoting culture, consumption and community awareness—such as *Main Line Today*—local history now commands an ever-expanding audience. It also seems to affirm the old proverb that all history is local history.

Mark Dixon's new book exemplifies the best traditions of the genre. It introduces readers to a world they thought they knew from *The Philadelphia Story* on stage and screen but, in fact, hardly know at all. Dixon's Main Line is more than a place of lace-curtained mansions, cricket clubs and horse shows where the rich display their wealth and servants bow and curtsy and appear as backdrops rather than individuals with their own lives and interests. Dixon's Main Line extends beyond the Welsh-named train stops such as Bala Cynwyd, Bryn Mawr and outward to include streetcar suburbs west and north from Philadelphia, mill towns along the Schuylkill River, horse farms in Chester County and new developments cropping up in fields with realtors' and boosters' promises of the best schools and all the creature comforts of prefabricated construction.

More than places, Dixon introduces readers to a cast of Main Line people as varied as athletes and attorneys, painters and preachers, native-born and immigrant and more. And he shows that living in a comfortable complacency was impossible because some of the very institutions that bespoke Main Line privilege, such as its liberal arts colleges and "main line" Protestant churches, brought in young women to learn how to organize the poor, women's rights reformers to remake the nation's politics and make over its governments, antiwar activists to end the Vietnam War and civil rights advocates to free the nation from its bondage to racism. The promise of privacy and prestige also brought in newly rich people, even instant millionaire ballplayers, whose lifestyles shook up the "old money" ambience of tony neighborhoods. The famous and a few of the infamous show up in Dixon's Main Line tellings and suggest in their variety that only by getting down to cases can one really know the Main Line—or any place. Image is not reality, as the local history reveals.

Dixon's Main Line was, and is, a dynamic place where many of the basic questions of community-making in America get their due: to preserve the once grand property or tear it down for a development project; to keep outsiders at arm's length or welcome them; to pile up wealth or use it for the common good. The Main Line was, and remains, a very connected place to the wider world. Its men and women went off to war—to fight or fight against it—and traveled the globe in quests of archaeological and artistic discovery. What they collected in ideas, experiences and sacred relics helped make the Main Line cosmopolitan, even worldly wise, even as some of its people sought to insulate themselves from the "problems" of others not like them. Some among the privileged class used their education and advantage to champion such fundamental liberties as free speech, while others measured the costs of intercollegiate sports in tallying the value of a higher education. Main Line people, in Dixon's telling, went down with the *Titanic*, sold a bridge to the British that allowed them to take Sudan, led the forces in Korea and marched with "Arnie's Army" on the golf course. And more. In all of this, Dixon's Main Line is really America's "Main Street." As such, its history becomes "our history," which, after all, is what the best local history can and must do.

Randall M. Miller
Saint Joseph's University

Acknowledgements

Among people interested in local history, libraries and librarians still rule. Even in 2010, no Internet search engine can produce the indenture that sent ten-year-old Phillis Ganges to work for a Philadelphia ironmonger in 1800 or the passionate conversation that filled the student newspaper when Haverford College abandoned football in the early 1970s. Those things exist only in libraries. So here is to libraries and librarians. They get too little appreciation and too little money. But among those who would know, they get a lot of love. And I mean you specifically, Jerry Francis of the Lower Merion Historical Society, Diane Rofini and Pam Powell of the Chester County Historical Society, Bennett Hill of the Radnor Historical Society and Lorett Treese of the Bryn Mawr College Archives, plus many others.

Thanks also to Mark Nardone, former editor of *Main Line Today* magazine, for giving me the column in which these stories were first published.

1740
FORGETTING "CYMRAEG"

Your neighbor doesn't speak English. You do. Is that a problem?
    Local history suggests that it needn't be. Language was not an issue for the region's Welsh settlers who, three centuries ago, were a majority of those who lived in Radnor and Tredyffrin Townships. Suffering no persecution and eventually developing other priorities—commerce, English-speaking marriage partners and religion—the Welsh themselves lost interest in the language and culture of their native land.

In Tredyffrin, the Reverend David Evans (circa 1681–1751) was hounded from his Presbyterian pulpit in 1740. His congregation didn't care that he was the only Welsh-speaking minister for three thousand miles. They disliked his theology, so replaced him with another minister. Never mind that the new minister spoke only English.

"For most, it appears that cultural and linguistic separateness was too high a price to pay for being locked out of the opportunity of becoming upward mobile young colonials," wrote historian Boyd Stanley Schlenther.

Initially, the Welsh immigrants had every intention of remaining Welsh. In 1681, a group of Welsh Quakers cut a deal with William Penn for a forty-thousand-acre tract (basically Merion, Haverford, Radnor and Tredyffrin Townships), "within which all causes, quarrels, crimes and disputes might be tried and wholly determined by officers, magistrates and juries of our own language." By 1700, "Cymraeg" was the dominant language in the so-called Welsh Tract.

The Welsh who founded Great Valley Presbyterian Church hoped to preserve their language and culture. But in 1740, they replaced Welsh-speaking Reverend David Evans with another minister whose theology they liked better but who spoke only English. *Chester County Historical Society.*

That Penn agreed to this proves, said Schlenther, that there was little prejudice against those who did not speak English. But the split with the Mother Country began early.

Many Welsh settlers already spoke English fluently, and others used the long sea voyages to learn it. News of the safe arrival of the first shipload of settlers was sent back to Wales in a letter written in English. Quaker services were bilingual from the start, and Quaker records were always in English.

Then, there was the griping from home. Immigration to Pennsylvania had made Quakerism almost extinct in Wales.

"By 1698, hot letters were being exchanged between Welsh Quakers of Wales and Pennsylvania, with the Wales Welsh critical of their Pennsylvania brethren for departing for newer pastures," wrote Schlenther. "Such criticism likely increased the readiness of the Pennsylvania Welsh Quakers to merge into their predominantly English surroundings."

Raised on a farm in Carmarthenshire, Evans first worked as an apprentice shepherd and weaver. He received only two or three years of formal education, but that—or possibly the experience of herding sheep—excited a desire to learn. So, in 1704, he "voyaged over the great seas to Pennsylvania to earn money so that I could buy plenty of books."

In Philadelphia, Evans's indenture was purchased by an English-speaking farmer from Merion. Evans went to work "patiently cutting trees and clearing the land, with very little opportunity to look at books." He also picked up carpentry skills, which helped pay off his indenture early.

In 1708, Evans moved to New Castle, where he worked as a carpenter, though "with little enjoyment" due to the inhabitants' "low morals." He moved on to Philadelphia but soon "wearied of that lively city." By 1710, Evans was living in Radnor, among his Welsh-speaking countrymen for the first time in six years.

In the former Welsh Tract, the early settlers from Wales are remembered mostly on road signs. The Welsh had hoped to perpetuate their culture, but as it turned out, their children preferred English spouses and upward mobility. *Mark E. Dixon.*

In Tredyffrin, Evans began leading religious services for a loosely organized group of Welsh Presbyterians with no resident minister. This drew the attention of the newly (1706) organized American Presbyterian Church, which censured Evans for "invading ye work of the ministry." Among Presbyterians, who traditionally valued an educated and ordained clergy, most ministers were graduates of Harvard or the University of Glasgow.

Rather than give up this interesting new work, Evans promptly became the American Presbyterians' first ministerial candidate. After first studying under local English-speaking ministers, he entered Yale and, with just one year of study, graduated in 1713. Ordained the following year, Evans was assigned to a Welsh congregation in Pencader (now Glasgow), Delaware.

Things did not go well. Almost from the start, Evans had "opinionative" differences with members of the congregation. The nature of the arguments was not recorded. Evans claimed that "the Devil with his devious tricks lit a bonfire of plots against me." He returned to Tredyffrin in 1718, "weak and faint" due to so much "wrangling and arguing." In 1723, he became the permanent minister at Tredyffrin.

Meanwhile, as American Presbyterianism became more organized, pressure grew to require that clergy endorse the Westminster Confession of Faith, a detailed, thirty-three-chapter theological statement created by church leaders in a 1643–47 conference at London's Westminster Abbey. Formal acceptance of the statement, supporters believed, would bring doctrinal conformity.

Evans objected. Such demands were normal in Scotland, where Presbyterianism was the official religion. In Wales, Presbyterians were dissenters and wary of creeds. When the church voted in 1727 to require ministers' signatures, Evans was among four to refuse. He remained outside the synod until 1730 and then declared "his hearty Concern for his withdrawal and desired to be received in as a member again."

Deciding to fight from the inside, Evans took advantage of a wording in the rules that allowed verbal acceptance of the Westminster document. Every other minister had signed.

Evans seems to have felt that a minister should be the leader of a congregation, not an underling who recited predigested formulas. The church, he wrote in 1731, must appoint only men whom it can "trust and hope to be truly gracious and holy men." But rather than expect emotional public outbursts or subscription to creeds, the church should leave "the searching of their Hearts unto God and themselves."

In 1732, Evans published—and Benjamin Franklin printed *The Minister of Christ, and the Duties of his Flock*, attacking Great Awakening "prattle against human learning in a minister of Christ, yet we are sure that learning and religion ever did, and do, fall or flourish together." Also that year, Franklin printed Evans's *A HELP for Parents* to instruct children in religious principles.

True, he had endorsed the Westminster Confession. But Evans's publication of his own catechism suggests that he considered it insufficient and himself qualified to provide what was missing. Evans's books were printed in English and included no references to Wales or Welsh culture. Apparently, he no longer considered himself a "Welsh" minister.

Meanwhile, there was strife in Tredyffrin. In 1739, one parishioner leveled unrecorded charges. In 1740, another accused Evans of teaching unorthodox (and unspecified) principles. In response, Evans removed all elders and deacons and attempted to rule the congregation alone. When members complained, the presbytery found no unorthodoxy but still transferred Evans to Pilesgrove, New Jersey.

Evans had the last word. For his farewell, he entered the pulpit and preached this, his full sermon: "Goats I found you, and goats I leave you."

Then, he left "the bitter wrangling of my own countrymen," the Welsh, and "crossed the Delaware by boat to Pilesgrove in pleasant New Jersey to preach Jesus Christ to the English."

Well, not entirely English. In Salem County, Evans's congregants included Germans, French, Irish and, especially, Dutch immigrants who worshiped together in a unity never apparent in Evans's Welsh pastorates. After eight years in Pilesgrove, Evans wrote that God had so "chained up the father of all strife so that he has not been able to stir up trouble here as he did formerly amongst my own countrymen."

Evans's replacement did not bring peace. During John Rowland's residence, the Tredyffrin church split into evangelical and nonevangelical factions. Finally, the nonevangelicals rallied their forces and locked the doors against Rowland and his supporters. The evangelicals built a new church at Charlestown.

In 1745, Evans's son, Samuel, also a Presbyterian minister, was assigned to the nonevangelical remnant of the church that his father had served. After six years, however, Samuel Evans deserted his wife and family and journeyed to England to seek ordination in the Church of England. David Evans blamed the quarrelsomeness of the Tredyffrin Welsh for his son's "black worries" so that "he wasted away and melancholy overcame him." In Evans's view, his countrymen had driven Samuel mad.

"We know nothing of his hurt or pain," wrote Evans near the end of his life in a poem composed in seventeenth-century Welsh. "If he is still alive, Oh Heavenly Father, keep him in thy Hand in the ways of peace."

Seven years after Samuel Evans's departure, the Tredyffrin congregation had still found no Welsh-speaking minister to replace him. So, the synod did what it had once refused to do: lower its educational standards. In 1758, it ordained John Griffith, a native of Wales, even "tho he has not the Measure of School Learning usually required, and which they judge to be ordinarily requisite." After Griffith died in 1770, many congregants drifted to the Charlestown church. In 1791, the two churches reunited as the Great Valley Presbyterian Church, which survives today.

Should the Welsh and other minorities have been pressured to give up their languages? Benjamin Franklin thought so. Writing of the Germans in 1751, Franklin asked, "Why should the Palatine Boors be suffered to swarm into our Settlements and, by herding together, establish their Language and Manners, to the Exclusion of Ours?" He favored denying Germans the right to vote until they learned English.

In 2000, according to the U.S. Census, 3.4 million people—about 1 percent of the population—couldn't speak English, up from 1.2 million in 1980. That worried some politicians, who have proposed legislation to make English the nation's official language. So far, those efforts have been mostly unsuccessful.

For most of us, it seems, strange languages are still no threat.

1800

PHILLIS'S STORY

Facts are facts. But history is largely about how facts are interpreted and by whom. So, here are some facts.

In 1800, the USS *Ganges*, an American warship, seized two American-owned vessels off Cuba. The *Prudent* and the *Phebe* were both illegally engaged in the slave trade. The proof was the presence of 135 Africans found naked and chained on board. The ships were sailed to Philadelphia and confiscated. The Africans were signed to apprenticeships with white Philadelphia-area families—many of them antislavery Quakers—and gradually melted into the region's growing population of free blacks.

So, was this a great victory in the long fight against slavery—or something less?

"Less" seems to have been the conclusion of Phillis Ganges Burr (died 1872), one of the Africans. Burr's version of the story, told to her friends and later inscribed on her tombstone at Devon's Great Valley Baptist Church, is this: "Born in Africa, brought to America in the slave ship Ganges and sold into slavery to pay for her passage and died April 18, 1872, aged nearly 100 years."

According to official records, this is almost completely wrong. First, her age may be off by as many as twenty years. Second, the *Ganges* was the rescue ship; the *Phebe* and *Prudent* were the slave ships. And third, Burr wasn't sold into slavery. She got an apprenticeship. Didn't she understand the difference?

Perhaps not, because her perspective seems plain: "I was not rescued!"

The USS *Ganges* was one of the first regular warships of the U.S. Navy. Built in 1794 for the West Indies trade, the *Ganges* was purchased by the

Erected by friends at Devon's Great Valley Baptist Church, the tombstone of Phillis Burr probably relates her view that the 1800 seizure by the USS *Ganges* of a slave ship bringing her from Africa was no rescue. *Mark E. Dixon.*

federal government in 1798 and converted to a man-of-war to protect U.S. shipping from French privateers. When *Ganges* first sailed from Philadelphia in May 1798, it was the first U.S. warship to put to sea since the Continental navy's last ship, the *Alliance*, had been sold in 1785.

Slavery was still legal in the United States. The institution had been abolished in northern states, though more quickly in some than in others. In 1780, Pennsylvania had passed a gradual abolition law that, by 1800, had reduced the number of slaves in the state to 1,706. Southern states, however, continued to legally import slaves until the slave trade was banned in 1808. (The trade continued illegally until the Civil War.)

At the federal level, Congress had been the recipient of mostly Quaker petitions to abolish the slave trade since it first convened in 1789. Those petitions were ignored. But in 1794, Congress threw antislavery activists a

Immigrants suspected of carrying infectious diseases were quarantined at the Essington Lazaretto from 1800 until the 1890s. The Ganges Africans were among the facility's first inmates. *Library of Congress.*

bone: the Federal Slave Trade Act prohibited the outfitting of slave ships in U.S. ports. Foreign ships could still bring slaves in, but U.S. ships could not.

Despite southern sensitivity on the issue of slavery, the bill passed with little opposition. Most opponents of slavery were northerners, and most U.S. slave ships were based in northern ports. Perhaps southerners reasoned that the measure was no skin off their noses.

Absence of a navy, however, made the law nearly impossible to enforce. That changed with the arrival of the *Ganges*.

The *Ganges'* primary mission was to protect American merchant ships. But on July 19, 1800, while escorting a convoy to Havana, it encountered the *Prudent* and, two days later, the *Phebe*. The ships were crowded with captives from Guinea, destined for a well-known slave trader at Havana. *Ganges* captain John Mullowny put prize crews aboard both ships and ordered them to sail for Philadelphia.

Charleston, South Carolina, and Savannah, Georgia, were closer, so Mullowny's choice of Philadelphia seems significant.

"Capt. Mullowny didn't have to send those ships all the way back here," said V. Chapman-Smith, administrator of the regional branch of the National Archives, which mounted a 2005 exhibit on the ships' capture. He did so, she theorized, because the *Ganges'* Philadelphia-based captain and crew had absorbed the city's antislavery sentiment.

According to historian Garry Wills, it was Philadelphia's antislavery sentiment and activism that, during the 1787 Constitutional Convention, caused southern politicians to insist on moving the U.S. capital out of the city. Three of George Washington's slaves escaped during his presidential term.

In August, when the first slave ship arrived at the quarantine station, the Lazaretto, in Delaware County, the U.S. marshal had no resources to care for so many people. Appalled by the slaves' condition, the Pennsylvania Anti-Slavery Society (PAS) and black leaders put out a call in the *Pennsylvania Gazette*:

> *Arrived at the Lazaretto yesterday, 118 Black People, without the least cloathing, being taken on board the schooner Phebe, prize to the United States ship Ganges. The humane citizens are requested to send to the Health-Office, at the State House, any kind of linen clothes for their accommodation, as well as to prevent the shock their decency will be exposed to by so many of both sexes being thus exposed naked.*

From Philadelphia to Malvern

In August 1800, 135 naked, chained Africans found aboard two slavers by the USS *Ganges* arrived at Essington's newly built Lazaretto, where officials spent $352.15 to nurse them back to health and to bury six who had died. *Library of Congress.*

Officials at the Lazaretto carefully recorded what was spent, $352.15, to nurse the Africans back to health and to bury six who died. That expense was probably charged against the value of the ships and may explain why there was no effort to send the Africans home. Perhaps there was no money left.

But at least the Africans were not deemed to be slaves. Instead, the U.S. District Court appointed PAS their legal guardian, responsible for easing the transition into American society of people who mostly spoke no English and had few skills. For legal purposes, PAS gave all of the Africans the surname "Ganges" and then signed them to indentures with farmers, shop owners and other employers throughout the region. In exchange for their labor, the whites promised to provide the Africans with food, clothing, shelter and an education.

Gradually, they dispersed. A boy, Bellor Ganges, went with Priscilla Mitchener of Philadelphia for twelve years, with a promise that he would learn the "Art & Mystery" of farming and receive "three quarters day schooling"—that is, schooling for three quarters of his daylight hours. Sambo Ganges was signed for four years, during which Mitchener promised to "use the utmost of her endeavors to teach him to read & write."

Mark Willcox, a papermaker in Concord Township, Delaware County, took Darrah Ganges, aged "about forty years," to learn "housewifery" and Tambo Ganges, seventeen, to learn farming. Silve Ganges went with Isaac Kirk of Upper Dublin, Montgomery County, to learn housewifery.

John Parker of Kennett Square took home young David Ganges, but the boy sickened and died despite bleedings and purgings with cream of tartar. He was buried at the Kennett meetinghouse, a scene Parker described in a letter published in the *West Chester Local* in 1884: "We were attended to his grave by six of his shipmates, namely Dabon, Sarrow, Nantilly, Moro, Sandalia and Gango, all New Africans, besides a small number of my beloved friends. He is happy I have no doubt. His native innocence and simplicity very much endeared him to me."

Two centuries later, telephone listings still include several dozen Ganges families, all in the Philadelphia region.

Also among the indenture papers—preserved at the Historical Society of Pennsylvania—is that of "Phillis Ganges," who went home with John William Godfrey, a Philadelphia ironmaster who promised that she would learn "housewifery" and receive both an education and her upkeep in exchange for eight years of labor. Phillis's indenture, like those of the other Africans, also pledged her not to marry, gamble, damage her master's goods, commit fornication, leave without permission or loiter around taverns or playhouses. Neither Phillis's indenture nor those of the other Africans indicate their assent to these arrangements; the documents are signed only by the employers and PAS representatives.

That Phillis Ganges and Phillis Burr were the same person is not certain. PAS indentures specified terms of four or five years for adults; boys were expected to work until the age of twenty-one and girls, until eighteen. Since Phillis Ganges was given an eight-year indenture, she was presumably about ten years old. That would make her eighty-two—not "nearly 100 years"— when Phillis Burr died in 1872. In 1850, however, Phillis Ganges would have been about sixty, which was close to the age (fifty-eight) recorded for Phillis Burr on that year's U.S. census. It may also be relevant that families named Godfrey lived in both Philadelphia and Tredyffrin Township at about the turn of the nineteenth century. Phillis Burr is buried in Tredyffrin.

Phillis Burr's husband—if she had one—is unknown. It is possible that she had some relation with the African American family long rumored to have been sired during an affair between Colonel Aaron Burr (1756–1836) and his black housekeeper during the Valley Forge encampment of 1777–78.

But the viewpoint on Phillis Burr's tombstone was not simply an aberration. At least one other African felt the same way. In 1892, a Kennett newspaper published an account of the life of "Old Dabbo" Ganges, who was indentured to Joseph Taylor of West Chester. After completing his indenture, Dabbo worked in the neighborhood raking hay and bleaching linen until he died about 1840. Fifty years later, according to the author, those who knew Dabbo still remembered him categorizing the *Ganges* as a "sea dungeon." Not the *Phebe* and not the *Prudent*; the *Ganges*—the rescue ship.

Which, said Chapman-Smith, is fair. "The Africans had free lives before being pulled onto a slave ship," she said. "The fact that they were rescued by the Navy didn't change the fact that they were taken to a strange place, 'sold' by the court and told to go to work to earn back the freedom that had been taken away from them."

And those, Phillis might have said, are the facts.

1884

LIBERALS AT WAR

War leaders need planes and ships and men, but they also need liberals. Hardware and soldiers can defeat armies, but only liberals have the soft skills required to brainwash defeated populations.

Doubt it? Consider postwar Germany, where de-nazification never really took hold until economic reforms and the Marshall Plan (administered by liberals) allowed its economy to recover. Or the Philippines, which resisted our 1898 takeover until we captured Filipinos' hearts by founding a university and sending a thousand teachers to set up local schools.

Earlier in the nineteenth century, Washington turned Indian affairs over to "Social Gospel" liberals who had criticized plans to make "good" (i.e., dead) Indians of the western tribes. Instead, church groups used schools to launder Indian children's minds to resemble those of little Caucasians. When Sitting Bull (1831–1890) visited Ponemah, an Indian school in Wayne, in 1884, he was not impressed.

Ponemah was the summer campus of the Lincoln Institution, an Indian school on South Eleventh Street in Philadelphia. Founded in 1866 to educate orphans of men killed in the Civil War, Lincoln Institute reinvented itself in the 1880s and, by 1884, had enrolled 103 girls and 99 boys from fifteen different tribes. More than half were Sioux.

"The Managers...determined to devote their energies to educating the Indians," declared Lincoln's 1884 annual report, "and thereby attempt the solution of one of the most important problems of the day."

Sitting Bull may have been underwhelmed by the Indian school that, for two summers in the 1880s, used the Spread Eagle Tavern in Wayne. Such schools saved his people from extermination but wiped out their culture. *Radnor Historical Society.*

The Indians became a "problem" after the Civil War, when tribes who had allowed immigrants to pass through the Dakotas, Colorado and New Mexico began to resist permanent settlement. The most serious conflict was in Montana, where the Sioux repeatedly attacked crews building the Bozeman Trail across tribal lands.

In 1869, Ulysses S. Grant came into office with a plan. "Much impressed with the humane ideas of the Quakers," according to the *Boston Advertiser*, he asked members of the denomination to serve as Indian agents. Noting that Quakers had had good relations with Indians as far back as William Penn, Grant hoped that their presence would make reservation life more attractive. Initially popular, this plan was abandoned after a few years when other denominations complained that they, too, should have a piece of the action. Thereafter, agents were appointed from all Protestant denominations, which were also allowed to establish churches and schools. Catholic missionaries received access in 1880.

Beyond the competition for souls, the church people—Quakers, too—agreed that Indian culture should be suppressed through education. Most Indian parents wanted their children to be literate but resisted the schools' cultural mission.

"Day schools failed…because they were day schools," wrote A.T. Andreas, author of an 1882 history of Nebraska. "The parents, having the scholars under their influence except during the few hours they were in school each day, exerted more power for evil than the teachers could for good."

Whites responded with nonreservation schools, pioneered by U.S. Army jailer Richard Henry Pratt (1840–1924), who had spent three years guarding Plains Indian prisoners in Florida. During this period, he "civilized" the Indians by putting them in military uniforms, cutting their hair and forcing them to speak English. A year after their release, Pratt founded Carlisle (Pennsylvania) Indian School on similar principles.

At first, children went to Carlisle voluntarily. Later, parents were coerced to give them up. "I would withhold…rations and supplies," said Thomas Jefferson Morgan, commissioner of Indian Affairs. "And when every other means was exhausted…I would send a troop of U.S. soldiers, not to seize them, but simply to be present as an expression of the power of the government. Then I would say to these people, 'Put your children in school; and they would do it.'" In 1895, some Hopi parents were imprisoned at Alcatraz for hiding their children.

Perhaps word had gotten out that the schools were no picnic. When Lone Wolf, a Blackfoot, arrived in the 1890s, he was stripped of clothes, belongings and his hair, all of which were burned. "Even the little medicine bags our mothers had given to us to protect us from harm," he recalled later. "Everything was placed in a heap and set afire. All of the buckskin clothes had to go and we had to put on the clothes of the white man." Indian names were replaced with white names chosen by teachers. The children were required to join a Christian church and forbidden to speak native languages.

"One evening…one of the boys said something in Indian to another boy," remembered Lone Wolf. "The man in charge…pounced on the boy, caught him by the shirt and threw him across the room," breaking his collarbone. The boy's father took the child and went to live in Canada.

Carlisle's curriculum oozed white superiority. "The books told how bad the Indians had been to the white men—burning their towns and killing their women and children," said Sun Elk of Taos Pueblo in 1890. "But I had seen white men do that to Indians."

Pratt's stated goal was to "kill the Indian, and save the man." And on a certain level, the system worked: Indian families and culture were damaged. When Anna Bender, a Chippewa, returned to Minnesota after seven years, she found herself not quite Indian and not quite white. "[My father] talked to me kindly and tried to help me recall my early childhood, which proved unsuccessful," she said. "At last he told me I had changed greatly from a loving child to a stranger and seemed disappointed which only added to my lonesomeness."

Between 1879 and 1918, more than ten thousand Indian children attended Carlisle, which also funneled students to Lincoln. Official descriptions of Lincoln activities—intended primarily to reassure donors—are glowing. In 1890, Robert Blight, chaplain, described students as "models [of] docility, gentleness…and good-temper." They worked with "diligence and interest." The girls made their own clothes. The boys learned trades and farming and made brooms, "which sell well." Blight also triumphantly noted the baptism of twenty-eight girls in the Episcopal church, with which Lincoln was affiliated.

Lincoln praised students' potential—they were "intelligent"—but also dripped with cultural condescension. If they were sickly, officials blamed the primitive conditions in which they were raised. If students were disinterested, the cause was the lack of intellectual curiosity "natural to" Indian culture. In 1888, Thomas J. Mays, MD, of Philadelphia reported to the county medical society that, based on his studies of eighty-two Lincoln girls, Indians were sickly because their breathing was incorrect.

"Abdominal [breathing] is the original type of respiration in both male and female," wrote Mays. "Costal [breathing] in the civilized female is acquired through the constricting influence of clothing around the abdomen."

Lincoln's Wayne program was announced in the spring of 1884, when the *Daily Local News* reported that the derelict Spread Eagle Tavern—now the site of Eagle Village Shops—had been lent to the school by George W. Childs, developer of north Wayne.

Philanthropists Mary and J. Belangee Cox paid for repairs and new furniture. Books were brought from the city, and the Pennsylvania Railroad agreed to transport the children for free. The reason for all this wasn't specified, but it may have been at least partially financial; the students were put to work growing vegetables, producing one hundred bushels of potatoes, twenty-five bushels of onions, 250 baskets of tomatoes and one thousand ears of corn. They also presented at least two concerts at the Wayne Lyceum, raising about $700.

Lincoln used the tavern for two seasons. After Childs demolished the building in 1886, the Coxes provided land near their country estate, Ivycroft, in Tredyffrin to erect new facilities.

Enthusiasm for the school's work was mixed. When the girls ventured north of Conestoga Road for a July Fourth picnic, a *Local* article bitingly observed the irony of the occasion. "The recollection of their parents under guard of rifle in a few thousand acres of western land," said the unsigned article, "will possibly inspire them to be thankful for the white man's independence and hopeful for their own."

Meanwhile, Sitting Bull was on the road. After the Custer massacre in 1876, the Sioux holy man had lived in Canada for five years before finally agreeing to live on South Dakota's Standing Rock Reservation. However, he retained every bit of his charisma—so much so that the local Indian agent considered him an obstacle to the goals of the reservation. When William "Buffalo Bill" Cody proposed that Sitting Bull join his Wild West Show for the 1884 season, the agent said, "Go."

"He drew tremendous crowds," according to historian Dee Brown, but may have been too naïve to understand show business. In Philadelphia, after Sitting Bull spoke in Lakota about the need for peace and education, a white man stood to "translate" his lurid description of the Battle of Little Big Horn.

On October 15, Sitting Bull alighted at the Wayne train station and was met by the entire student body and a niece, with whom, said the *Local*, he had "a good hugging time." Mary Cox gave Sitting Bull and the other chiefs pipes and tobacco. Back at the tavern, they feasted at long tables, after which the chief watched without comment as the children sang Episcopal hymns, marched in formation like soldiers and recited the writings of white men.

"He thought it was a nice place," reported the *Local*, "but mentioned that the fathers of the children were being starved a little now and then out on the frontier."

The liberals' solution, in other words, was better than extermination—but not by a lot.

1885
EAKINS (SORT OF) COMES OUT

Thomas Eakins (1844–1916) wasn't subtle. When the painter decided to announce his sexual leanings, he did it loudly—with an 1885 painting of six men standing, sitting, diving (*naked*) on a stone pier jutting into Bryn Mawr's Dove Lake.

And lest his viewers miss the point, Eakins himself appears in *Swimming*. Neck deep in the lake, Eakins is swimming toward the pier with his eyes fixed just *there* on one of his companions.

That's how some see it. In fact, nobody knows which way Eakins swung. The artist loved the human form—the *entire* human form, of *both* genders! Perhaps this was his way of teasing the narrow-minded—which, compared to Eakins, was just about everyone.

Today, gay historians point to *Swimming* as evidence that Eakins was one of them—even, writes Eakins biographer William S. McFeely, "to the point of triumphantly insisting on a sight line from Eakins to the diver's penis." Eakins's contemporaries weren't blind to this, but nineteenth-century standards made it difficult to comment. Instead, critics ignored what has since been called America's "most accomplished rendition of the nude figure." Rejected by the patron who commissioned it, *Swimming* was shoved into a closet until 1925, when Eakins's widow sold it to a Fort Worth, Texas museum.

Born in Philadelphia, Eakins was the eldest child of a respected instructor of penmanship at Friends Central. Benjamin Eakins was never rich. But with thrift and savvy investments, he built an estate that allowed his son to study in Paris and, later, defy artistic conventions.

Thomas Eakins's *Swimming* was based on studies at Dove Lake in Bryn Mawr. According to many art and gay historians, the work is proof that the artist—who included himself at lower right—was homosexual. *Lower Merion Historical Society.*

The Eakinses seem to have been freethinkers. Eakins's mother, Caroline, was raised a Quaker and Benjamin, a Presbyterian. But there is no evidence that Thomas Eakins's parents attended religious services after their marriage. Still, they "clearly incorporated Quaker values in their household," wrote biographer Sidney D. Kirkpatrick, who listed among the family's virtues "self discipline" and "a hatred of hypocrisy and pretension and a stubborn adherence to truth and honesty in the face of opposition."

After graduating from Central High in 1861, Eakins studied drawing and anatomy at the Pennsylvania Academy of Fine Arts. Later, he attended courses in anatomy and dissection at Jefferson Medical College and considered becoming a surgeon. From 1866 to 1870, Eakins studied at École des Beaux-Arts in Paris under the internationally known Jean-Leon Gerome. Gerome became Eakins's mentor, fostering an appreciation for realism and the nude.

"No pupil left without learning to perfectly draw the human form," wrote Kirkpatrick.

Gerome may also have contributed to the bluntness that characterized Eakins. It was the Frenchman's habit, wrote Kirkpatrick, to "look carefully and a long time at the model and then at the [student's] drawing, and then he will point out every fault." The point of sketching, said Gerome, was to master principles. He derided as "ladies' work" the time wasted on finishing drawings. In Paris, Eakins developed impatience with Victorian attitudes—the horror of nudity, for instance—that interfered with learning. This would eventually get him into trouble.

Writing to Benjamin Eakins in 1868, the artist stated his view: "She [the female nude] is the most beautiful thing there is in the world except a naked man but I never yet saw a study of one exhibited…It would be a godsend to see a fine man model painted in the studio with the bare walls, alongside of the smiling smirking goddesses of waxy complexion."

Eakins returned to Philadelphia in 1870, intending to make a living as a portraitist. His timing was good. Philadelphia was booming with new wealth. In every direction, successful businessmen were erecting mansions whose walls needed covering. On the downside, their tastes were often provincial.

"Painters were expected to embroider tedious reality by producing grandiose landscapes and flattering portraits in massive gilt frames," wrote Fitzpatrick. "The only rule was that paintings be pictorially pleasing, expressive of the pervading spirit of prosperity and optimism."

Eakins started by painting family and friends. It was good practice but brought no money. His first break came when a Union League exhibition accepted *Max Schmitt in a Single Scull*, a portrait of a champion rower who also happened to be a personal friend. Eakins chose the subject deliberately to show a prominent Philadelphian in a recognizable local setting—on the Schuylkill—and thereby court the attention of potential clients. Schmitt didn't row in the nude, but his light, sleeveless shirt revealed enough musculature to allow Eakins to demonstrate his skills.

Eakins won no awards and reviews were mixed. The *Philadelphia Inquirer* called the painting "scarcely satisfactory." The *Bulletin* used the word "peculiar" but predicted Eakins's "conspicuous future." That was enough; Eakins had been noticed. He gave the painting to Schmitt and moved on.

During his forty-year career, Eakins painted several hundred portraits, many of friends and family but also of prominent Philadelphians. Many had a distinct Eakins edge. His 1875 *Gross Clinic*, which depicted prominent surgeon Samuel D. Gross in mid-operation, was controversial both for the patient's naked hindquarters and the redness of the bloody scalpel. The artist's talent was undeniable, but in an era during which Americans thought undraped table legs shocking, Eakins's blunt realism troubled many.

Even so, the Pennsylvania Academy took a chance on Eakins's cutting-edge ideas. Inspired, perhaps, by its new (and also cutting-edge) Frank Furness building on North Broad Street, the academy added "life-drawing" (nude) classes to the curriculum. Eakins joined for additional practice and, eventually, took over. In 1879, he was named a professor and, in 1882, director of instruction.

Eakins's tenure probably caused many ulcers. He passionately believed that artists learned best by drawing nude models. This presumed that the academy's real purpose was to train artists and not be a finishing school for the children of high society.

And who should model? In theory, students could model for one another; in practice, models were often paid, and some were prostitutes. That male students should draw nude women was tolerable, but that women should see a nude male was scandalous. Yet Eakins insisted on treating male and female students as equals. By the early 1880s, despite itself, the academy's program was "the most liberal and advanced in the world."

But opportunities to depict nude subjects were few. It could be done in historical scenes. Gerome lived by painting Roman gladiators and slave girls. Eakins tried similar tricks. In 1877, he unveiled *William Rush Carving His Allegorical Figure of the Schuylkill River*, which depicted an earlier Philadelphia artist using a nude female model. But Eakins's desire was to paint the people and places of his time.

Eakins's interest in realism extended to sports, which produced his rowing and boxing pictures. Another was anatomy; Eakins's students dissected human and animal cadavers. Yet another was outdoor sketching. So, it was nothing unusual when, in 1884 and '85, Eakins and several students and assistants traveled to Dove Lake.

Located three miles northwest of the resort at Bryn Mawr, Dove Lake was named for the pre-revolutionary Dove Mill, which had made paper for the Continental Congress. The lake became a popular recreational site in the 1870s, when the owner dammed the creek. To many Philadelphians, Dove Lake was as recognizable as today's Jersey Shore.

Probably, the Eakins party walked from Bryn Mawr station to the lake. Opportunities to run, wrestle, lounge, swim and dive in the nude were rare, so Eakins made numerous photographs of the scene for reference back in his studio.

"Eakins was 'boss' to the students and ostensibly their supervisor, yet he also participated in some if not all of their activities," wrote Kirkpatrick. "He appears nude in three of the photographs."

Eakins's patron was academy trustee Edward Coates, who had offered the artist $800 for a painting whose subject Eakins was free to choose. Coates's only guidance was an expressed desire that the painting might eventually become part of the academy's collection. The offer may have been an unofficial way to boost Eakins's annual salary of $1,200.

What Coates didn't expect—and certainly didn't intend to hang over his mantle—was his foremost teacher skinny-dipping with his students. Coates was a conservative man, a financier who made his money in the cotton industry and invested in banks and insurance companies. He viewed his work with the academy as a form of philanthropy but does not seem to have been a serious art collector. Coates's preference was French landscapes. Nudity was tolerable if the figures were anonymous or lived in the distant past. But each of the six men in *Swimming* was an identifiable member of the academy's community.

Plus, it was politically inconvenient. Complaints about Eakins's methods had never stopped. "The painting could easily have been regarded as an aggressive statement of Eakins' teaching method," writes art historian Doreen Bolger. "Its purchase by Coates would have been read as his personal endorsement of Eakins' then-disputed academic program." Coates declined *Swimming* and took another painting instead.

A year later, Eakins's uneasy relationship with the academy came to a noisy conclusion when he removed a loincloth from a male model in front of female students. He might have survived that. But after a private meeting with five of Eakins's students—including Thomas Anschutz, who had taken some of the *Swimming* photos—Coates requested the artist's resignation.

What did they say? "Powerful circumstantial evidence points to the five's making an accusation that Eakins was an active homosexual," wrote McFeely. Such stories had circulated before *Swimming* gave them a tangible form. But now, faced with an actual accusation, the board was forced to act. "Publicly, officially, they could not countenance unmanly behavior by an instructor in the academy studios."

Was Eakins gay? There is no sure evidence either way. Thomas and Susan MacDowell Eakins's marriage lasted thirty-two years until his death. But that's not proof. The couple had no children. But that's not proof, either.

Whether the issue was nudity or homosexuality, what chafed most was that Eakins would not deny or apologize for what he was. So in the end, both amounted to the same thing.

1898

CAREY AND *MADAME X*

M ost of all, the powerful crave immortality. That's why the pharaohs left us sphinxes carved with their own faces and why Stalin erected statues of himself in nearly every Soviet village.

With the same impulse, but a much smaller budget, M. Carey Thomas (1857–1935) chose John Singer Sargent (1856–1925)—an artist, but not just any artist—to do her portrait, which still hangs in the college library. Proud to be a pioneer in women's higher education, Thomas thought Sargent's unconventional style was a good match for her unconventional womanhood.

Best remembered today for *Madame X*—the 1884 portrait that gave a Paris socialite a slutty image—Sargent preferred to paint independent women: suffragists, actresses, lesbians and society belles. He purposely avoided conservative women and housewives, which was exactly the sort of woman Thomas never wanted to be.

"I don't like them," Sargent told a friend. "They are too like your well-to-do, respectable, middle-class women going to church on a Sunday afternoon." Carey Thomas's attitude exactly.

Born in Baltimore, Martha Carey Thomas ultimately rejected most tenets of organized religion. Instead, she embraced a form of social Darwinism, which held that society should be led and protected by its best people. Unlike her parents—who defined "best" as Christians, preferably other Quakers— Thomas favored the educated, the wealthy and, especially, those who appreciated "beauty"—the arts, literature and knowledge. Unlike many in her era, she envisioned an active role for women.

Never conventional, pioneer educator M. Carey Thomas chose John Singer Sargent—a painter who specialized in unconventional women—to do her portrait. Sargent obliged by highlighting Thomas's serious face, emphasizing her intelligence in an era that didn't much value female intellect. *Bryn Mawr College.*

Thomas—who always went by Carey rather than her feminine first name—was conceived "in full daylight," according to a family story. Her mother, Mary Whitall Thomas, had previously miscarried. So, her father, James Carey Thomas, a physician, proposed having intercourse at midday, so conception would occur when both were "at the height of their physical powers." Mary Thomas wondered aloud for the rest of her life whether this had produced her daughter's "irrepressible" personality.

The Thomases wanted their daughter to be "born again," in the religious sense. When Carey was two, Mary Thomas recorded hopefully in her diary that she "made her first little prayer tonight. She asked Heavenly Father to give her a new little heart." But by age four, Carey was off the traces: as a joke, an aunt dressed her as a boy. Carey decided she liked it.

At age seven, she was severely burned in a kitchen accident and nearly died. Carey spent eighteen months in bed, enduring painful dressing changes that put an end to her childish faith. Her mother prayed over Carey's bed that her suffering might ease. But what the girl had observed was that the prayers didn't work.

"I felt sure that if my mother prayed hard enough, God would not let my dressings hurt me so awfully," Thomas later wrote. But "the pain never lessened [and] I knew that there must be something wrong with God."

As she grew older, Thomas increasingly dismissed the religious and gender-based restrictions that hemmed her in. When Mary Thomas rejected Carey's request for a set of science instruments, saying, "Oh, but you can't, you're *girls*," she and a friend immediately got to work and created a Leyden jar to create electricity. When James Thomas mentioned St. Paul's injunction that men were stronger and, therefore, should lead women, Carey wrote, "[I]t made me so mad, almost beside myself."

She crawled out windows and walked on roofs. By age fifteen, Carey had an unformed vision of a future dedicated to debunking both her father and St. Paul. She would not marry, which she believed required subservience. "If Heavenly Father spares me my senses, I'll never be dependent on anyone, man or woman, if possible," she wrote in her diary. "I am thoroughly and heartily women's rights and never expect to change my opinion."

To realize her dream, Carey focused on higher education. James Thomas was a lay Quaker minister, a fact that involved the family in church and community projects. Among these was the founding of Johns Hopkins University. So, as Carey was finishing her high school education in the 1870s, she thought she might attend this new school. But Johns Hopkins became an all-male school, so she chose Cornell, graduating in 1877 with a degree in literature.

The thrill of Carey's Cornell years occurred not on campus, but rather when she learned that her family was involved in establishing yet another college. A wealthy benefactor had proposed a Quaker college for women; Carey's father, uncle and cousin were helping to choose the site. The news crystallized Carey's career plans: the college would be the vehicle with which she would demonstrate the potential of women.

To gain control of the college, however, she would need both higher academic credentials and the appearance of being a good Quaker.

For the former, she headed to Switzerland, where in 1882 she earned a PhD in linguistics from the University of Zurich. Meanwhile, she campaigned. "It is best for the president of a woman's college to be a woman," she wrote James Rhoads, who headed the emerging college.

She offered recommendations regarding the size and qualifications of the faculty and the number of fellowships. She also offered herself, declaring that her success at Zurich qualified her "without presumptuousness" for the college presidency.

Meanwhile, Thomas obscured her religious skepticism. "Thee knows I have an affection for the Society of Friends which an outsider could never feel," she wrote her mother. "I believe its views are more in accordance with the Bible than those of any other denomination." And this: "Personally, I like to go to meeting once a week. I believe it helps one." (In fact, in Thomas's three years abroad, she never once attended Quaker worship.)

As it turned out, the elderly Rhoads himself was named first president of Bryn Mawr. But that only meant a delay. In 1884, Thomas was named the first female college dean in the country. When Rhoads retired one decade later, Thomas replaced him and remained in the office until 1922.

Though not its first president, M. Carey Thomas left her stamp on Bryn Mawr. She saw it as a women's Leipzig, devoted to research and attracting great scholars. It was the first to organize study into a group system—a forerunner of the academic major—and prepared students for graduate work and significant (read: nonteaching) careers. It offered graduate education to women at a time when virtually no other U.S. colleges did.

"[Thomas] was a heroine in her prime, widely celebrated in the press," wrote biographer Helen Horowitz. "Of the important women of the time, she held a prominent and secure place."

Except among "Mawrters," though, her reputation has faded, in part due to her now unfashionable bigotries. Thomas's Bryn Mawr hired no Jewish or African American faculty, though it did admit Jewish students. When black educator Mary McLeod Bethune spoke at morning chapel in 1920, Thomas saw that she left on the morning train. Seating a black woman for lunch, she thought, "might cause difficulty."

On the other hand, Thomas was a dedicated suffragist—first president of the National College Women's Equal Suffrage League and an advocate for the National Woman's Party.

Such activities made the college suspect to conservatives. In 1904, for instance, T.E. Schmauk, a prominent Lutheran minister, told his church's general assembly that "[i]f I had a daughter to educate I should never think of sending her to that heathen institution at Bryn Mawr, where the students are told that Adam and Eve are myths." According to a newspaper account, many nodded.

Sargent was born in Florence, Italy, to American parents. Widely traveled in Europe, he never set foot in the United States until just before his twenty-first birthday, when he came back to retain his citizenship. Sargent began his career when his mother, an amateur artist, encouraged him to sketch. Mary Sargent insisted that he finish at least one drawing daily. Later, he studied formally in Italy, Germany and in Paris.

"He worked hard and with a uniformity of excellence astonishing even in a man so generously gifted," wrote art critic Thomas Craven. "He never missed a dimension, or varied a hairsbreadth from the exact size and just relationships of features; he was a dead shot at likenesses."

In 1882, when living in Paris, Sargent won a commission to paint Virginie Gautreau (1859–1915), an American expatriate known as one of the city's great beauties. It caused a scandal.

The enormous (eighty-two by forty-three inches) canvas, *Madame X*, showed Gautreau standing, clad in a strapless black dress that bared her shoulders and (almost) her chest, with one hand resting lightly on a table. Her pale skin, with the dark dress and background, only emphasized how much of it there was.

"The doors of the Salon were hardly open before the picture was damned," Sargent reported later. "The public took upon themselves to inveigh against the flagrant insufficiency, judged by prevailing standards, of the sitter's clothing." He thought it an odd criticism, given that Virginie's social position was based largely on showing her skin well. Another artist later painted straps on the dress. Sargent moved to England.

And that was where Thomas found him. In July 1899, she sat with Sargent for six days as he painted her portrait. The painting, which arrived at Bryn Mawr that October, shows Thomas in a dark academic robe with light on her serious face. The effect emphasizes her intelligence, which, in that era, was about as popular as showing her underdressed.

Whether Thomas appreciated that fundamental similarity to *Madame X* is unknown. But she loved the portrait and enthusiastically lent it for showings.

"I should very much like to have my portrait exhibited in Washington," she wrote the Corcoran Gallery in 1906. "So many people have the unjust impression that [Sargent] is incapable of painting the portrait of a woman as seriously as that of a man."

Immortality achieved.

1901

THE WORK OF THE LORD

Politics and religion mix fine. Politics and *ministers?* Not so much.

In 2005, evangelical minister (and former presidential candidate) Pat Robertson proposed that the United States "take out" (kill) Venezuelan president Hugo Chavez to avoid war with the country that supplied 12–15 percent of U.S. oil imports.

A century earlier, in 1901, a Frazer minister shocked those at a memorial service for freshly assassinated President William McKinley by observing that McKinley had it coming.

Like Robertson, Kelley's intent was purely humanitarian. The pastor of Frazer Presbyterian Church was a passionate prohibitionist who felt that McKinley had been a tool of the saloonkeepers. "I said nothing to condone the [assassination]," Kelley protested to a *Daily Local News* reporter after he was hanged in effigy.

Throughout the nineteenth century, activists had preached moderation in the consumption of alcohol—mostly without result. Now, most favored prohibition. The movement blamed many social ills—especially joblessness and domestic violence—on alcohol. In colonial America, despite annual per-capita alcohol consumption of 3.5 gallons, social and religious norms had made drunkenness unacceptable. After the Revolution, though, traditional norms faded. Poverty, unemployment and crime increased and were often blamed on alcohol.

After the Civil War, prohibition became a major issue in every political campaign from the presidency to the local school board. Prohibitionists organized dozens of local, state and national organizations. Most powerful were the Women's Christian Temperance Union (founded 1874) and the Anti-Saloon League (1893). Working through its Department of Scientific Temperance Instruction, the WCTU pioneered the child-oriented educational programs now used by secular groups such as DARE. By 1900, the WCTU had persuaded every state to pass legislation requiring anti-alcohol education.

What the league wanted was a final solution to the liquor question. ASL "has not come," said one leader, "simply to build a little local sentiment or to secure the passage of a few laws, or yet to vote the saloons from a few hundred towns. These are mere incidents in its progress. It has come to solve the liquor problem." The league's strategy was to enforce existing legislation and enact more until, finally, the saloons were exterminated.

Led by ministers, ASL encouraged the view that it was working God's will. Signers of its abstinence pledge were inducted into ASL's Lincoln-Lee Legion, which—supported by obscure quotations—argued that both Abraham Lincoln and Robert E. Lee had favored prohibition. This tactic allowed it to enlist supporters and raise money in both northern and southern churches.

The league's clout was first demonstrated in 1905 when it helped unseat an Ohio governor who had threatened to veto anti-alcohol legislation.

The cause provided a way for politicians to distinguish themselves. In 1870, McKinley himself used liquor control to make headlines in his first political office—prosecuting attorney of Stark County, Ohio. In the town of Alliance, McKinley indicted every saloonkeeper for selling to minors. Helping make the cases was Philander C. Knox, a student at Mount Union College whose frank testimony of his own past misdeeds impressed McKinley. When he came to the White House twenty-five years later, McKinley appointed Knox, then a corporate lawyer, as his attorney general.

McKinley's relations with anti-alcohol forces later soured. He served wine at state dinners and was an enthusiastic user of Vin Mariani, a French blend of wine and coca that contained a low level of cocaine. Other users included Queen Victoria and Pope Leo XIII, who awarded the company a Vatican medal and appeared on a poster endorsing the product.

Worse, McKinley obstructed efforts to dry out the armed forces, which then sold liquor by the drink at base canteens (mess halls). In 1899, after seizing Spain's empire—Cuba, Puerto Rico, Guam and the Philippines—Congress responded to the nation's assumption of the "white man's burden" by passing legislation to ensure that its occupation troops were sober. It ordered the canteens closed.

The WCTU dismissed claims that the closings were bad for morale or that the men would go off base to drink. "The American people still believe they are more powerful than the Army," observed the group's newspaper. "They will not sit idly by and let the Army crowd the theory down their throats that it takes liquor to make a good soldier." If soldiers got drunk in town, said the WCTU, they should be confined to their bases.

McKinley, however, declined to enforce the law, arguing through Attorney General Knox that it interfered with his authority as commander in chief.

Prohibitionists howled. "[McKinley] had been a constant disappointment to me," said Carrie Nation. "He was the brewers' president and did their biddings. We were willing to give our boys to fight the battles of this nation, to die in a foreign land, but we were not willing that a murderer [alcohol] should follow them from their home shores to kill their bodies and souls."

This was said at the height of the Philippine Insurrection. In 1898, Filipino patriots had hoped that America's victory in the Spanish-American War could lead to their independence. But when America occupied the country, Filipinos rebelled. By 1902, the conflict had killed more than 4,000 U.S. soldiers, 16,000 Filipino combatants and as many as 200,000 Filipino civilians.

But militarism, imperialism and heaps of battle dead didn't bother the "drys." In Detroit, Methodists rejoiced in U.S. dominance over these Catholic and non-Christian countries while mourning that Manila had more than a thousand saloons. "What Manila really needs," proclaimed the Methodists' 1900 Detroit Annual Conference, "is the establishment within her borders of the better elements of Americanism, such as business push, public spirit, municipal ambition, political integrity *and Protestant liberality and uprightness*" (emphasis added).

The 1900 platform of the Prohibition Party didn't even mention the war, though it ripped McKinley for ignoring the anti-canteen law: "President McKinley…has done more to encourage the liquor business, to demoralize the temperance habits of young men, and to bring Christian practices and requirements into disrepute, than any other President this republic has had."

Alford Kelley arrived on the Main Line in 1894 to assume the pastorates of both the Malvern and Frazer Presbyterian churches. (He preached at one and then rode his horse to the other for a later service.) Kelley came late to the ministry, graduating from Princeton in 1886 and its seminary in

1889. Kelley never married but instead resided with his mother and sister. Ordained by the Presbytery of Carlisle in 1890, his first assignment was Dickinson Presbyterian Church near Carlisle.

It is not known when Kelley joined the Anti-Saloon League, but he was clearly in sympathy when McKinley was shot by an anarchist on September 6, 1901, in Buffalo. The president died on the fourteenth. (His assassin, Leon Czolgosz, was indicted on September 16, convicted on the twenty-fifth and electrocuted on October 29.) September was a month filled with memorial services.

On Wednesday evening, September 18, Kelley and three other Baptist and Presbyterian ministers joined to lead a service in Malvern. What Kelley said apparently escaped a *Daily Local News* reporter, whose story the next day noted only that "the audience was very large and fully impressed with the spirit of the day." But others listened more closely and, on Saturday, the *Local* carried a page one story about a large "indignation meeting" called to assembly by a fife-and-drum corps at Malvern Presbyterian the previous evening.

Malvern Presbyterian was one of the churches Kelley had come to lead but with which he had apparently parted ways during the previous eight years. Most outraged, it seemed, were several former parishioners. One, H. Morgan Ruth, announced plans to carry the meeting's resolution against Kelley to the presbytery.

The next morning, a reporter knocked on the parsonage door and asked Kelley's version. Sitting on a wheelbarrow, the minister repeated his address from memory:

> *Why…have we met together? Because President McKinley, our chosen Chief Executive, represented law and authority, which God from the earliest times of our race, established on earth. President McKinley's assassin was an enemy of law, authority, humanity and God. We are here as representatives and defenders of law, authority, humanity and God.*
>
> *To quote the* New York Sun, *on "The Spirit of Anarchy," where, in the United States, law is defied, and for its processes, the will of individuals is substituted, there the spirit of assassination reigns.*
>
> *I dislike to introduce anything seemingly out of harmony with this meeting, and yet I have been thinking and cannot help now speaking of an instance in President McKinley's life which is of a similar character with the above conduct.*

Whilst sanctioning all that has been said with respect to the noble character of our martyred president, his nullification of law...in annulling the anti-canteen law, President McKinley has thus exhibited the spirit of anarchy.

If President McKinley, the Christian, educated, chief executive of our country, the leading exponent of law, can thus trample on one law, what can be expected of a Godless, ignorant, lawless man of the world [Czolgosz]? If one can defy law, why may not the other feel justified in his conduct?

Kelley wasn't the only one with a loose tongue. Anarchist Emma Goldman (1869–1940) called McKinley the "president of the money kings and trust magnates" and compared Czolgosz to Brutus, the assassin of Julius Caesar. She was widely reviled and spent a brief time in jail while officials tried to connect her to the murder.

In Frazer, some wanted to march on the parsonage. But in the end, the only action was that of a few boys who stuffed a dummy, labeled it "Rev. Kelley" and burned it in the street. Kelley preached at Frazer another four years and then left, complaining that he couldn't live on the $750 annual salary. He served briefly at a church in Erie and then quit the ministry to spend ten years helping lead the Pennsylvania Anti-Saloon League.

His most insightful remarks, however, may have been those that followed his sermon in October, one month after his big faux pas. Stepping from the pulpit, Kelley assured the congregation of his patriotism, adding that he felt like the apostle Paul, who once complained that the more he loved his people, the less he was loved.

"I trust, since I fall so far short of the great apostle," said Kelley, "that my explanation and avowal of affection may be as effective as his in removing all misunderstanding, that my love to you may be fully reciprocated and the work of the Lord not be hindered."

Pat Robertson couldn't have said it better.

COGS IN A WHEEL

L istening to politicians, one might think that same-sex marriage was something new. In fact, people have been making nontraditional "arrangements" since, well, forever.

From 1902–6, for instance, a stone farmhouse in Villanova was the scene of what gay rights activists insist—and evidence seems to support—was not one but two of that era's best-known such liaisons. Until evicted by a landlord objecting to their lifestyle, the women of the "Cogs" family lived happily and productively in what their contemporaries called "Boston" marriages.

The world benefited. The Cogs marriages provided three prominent artists with ready collaborators whose influence improved their work, which includes many murals at the state capitol in Harrisburg. In lieu of rent, a fourth partner assumed the household's domestic chores, thereby confounding the women's friend, journalist Anna Lea Merritt, who had written in 1900 that, "The chief obstacle to a woman's success is that she can never have a wife."

As it turned out, a woman could.

"Cogs" was an acronym formed from the surnames of Henrietta *C*ozens (1859–1940), Violet *O*akley (1874–1961), Elizabeth Shippen *G*reen (1871–1954) and Jessie Willcox *S*mith (1863–1935), who informally adopted it when they moved to the Red Rose Inn on Spring Mill Road. Oakley, Green and Smith had met in the Drexel Institute drawing classes of Howard Pyle. Cozens was not an artist, just a single woman who longed to be a homemaker without having to marry a man.

For four years, Villanova's Red Rose Inn was home to three prominent female artists whose "Boston" marriages caused tongues to wag in Victorian Philadelphia and got them evicted by a landlord who disliked their lifestyle. *Lower Merion Historical Society.*

C probably met O, G and S through friends.

Briefly engaged in 1888, Cozens broke it off after her fiancé criticized her lack of career direction; then she lived with Smith for almost fifty years. Green and Oakley's affair, however, ended in 1911 when Green married a man whom Oakley had considered a platonic friend. Tongues wagged after stories suggesting Oakley's despair appeared in local papers and again when she later took up with a young female student.

It was called a Boston marriage after Henry James's 1885 novel *The Bostonians*, which detailed a marriage-like relationship between two "New Women" who were independent, unmarried and self-supporting. Such women were considered new because, previously, women had only rarely held jobs. By the Cogs' time, though, U.S. society accepted this development. Even traditionalists conceded that the slaughter of 600,000 American men during the Civil War meant that many women would have to support themselves.

According to historian Lillian Faderman, such partners were often pioneers in the professions, suffragists and involved in cultural activities.

Boston marriages were not considered sexually perverted because proper Victorian women were believed to have almost no sex drive. Therefore, female romances were considered harmless almost by definition.

Life Was Made for Love and Cheer (1904), by Elizabeth Shippen Green, was among the artist's many works created as magazine illustrations in an era before photography was common. Green and three other women lived at Villanova's Red Rose Inn from 1902 to 1906. *Library of Congress.*

Lesbian historians, however, believe that many such relationships were physically sexual as well as conscious choices to avoid lifetime servitude to men. Seeming to confirm this is the fact that, about the time suffrage began to gain political traction, psychologists began to label intense female friendships as sick.

In 1902, a British sexologist warned of excessive attachments among female college students: "They kiss each other fondly on every occasion," wrote Havelock Ellis (1859–1939). "It is most natural, in the interchange of visits, for them to sleep together. They learn the pleasure of direct contact, and in the course of their fondling they resort to cunnilinguistic practices. After this a normal sex act fails to satisfy them."

Born in New York, Oakley later joked that she had entered the world with a paintbrush, not a silver spoon, in her mouth. Her parents, both grandfathers and two aunts were all accomplished painters, and Violet was encouraged in art. After an older sister died suddenly of diphtheria, however, her anxious parents kept Violet at home until she was twenty, copying engravings of the works of old masters that her grandfathers had brought back from Europe. Whatever it did for her skills, this isolation seems to have left her painfully shy.

Only in 1894 did Oakley begin her formal art education at the Art Students League in New York. The following year, her father's health began to fail and, with it, the family's finances. Looking for a practical career, Violet enrolled in Pyle's illustration class in 1896. Publishers then relied on artists, rather than photography, so training in illustration could lead to steady work.

Green was the child of Jasper Green, who had been an illustrator-correspondent for *Harper's Weekly* during the Civil War. The family wasn't rich but did have old Philadelphia social connections. Elizabeth's easy access to all levels of society probably contributed to her easygoing temperament and self-confidence. She was small, slim and described by one friend as "a delightful person, and full of fun, who didn't mind making herself look ridiculous."

Green never considered a career in fine art. Instead, like her father, she focused on illustration and, in 1889, was accepted for study at the Pennsylvania Academy of Fine Arts. She paid the eight-dollars-per-month tuition with money earned producing fashion illustrations for local newspapers. After graduating in 1893, Green worked for Strawbridge & Clothier and then the *Ladies' Home Journal*; she was among the working professionals who crowded Pyle's class in 1894.

There were no artists in the family of Jessie Smith, a Friends Central graduate whose first job had been teaching kindergarten. Smith stumbled into her true career while chaperoning a friend who was taking drawing lessons from a male teacher. Joining the lessons, Smith displayed natural ability. She soon quit her job—Smith found small children obnoxious anyway—and, in 1885, enrolled at the academy to study under Thomas Eakins. Smith considered Eakins, who was attracting criticism for insisting that female students draw nude men, a "madman."

Decorum was important to Smith, who hated conflict and scandal. She had had a happy childhood and would eventually make her reputation painting idyllic pictures of children. In 1894, however, she enrolled in Pyle's class, hoping to move beyond the need to sketch commercial illustrations of stoves and bars of soap.

Things clicked. Smith was impressed by Oakley's sophistication and Oakley, by Smith's competence and experience. On a personal level, Green's outgoing personality balanced Oakley's reticence, while Cozens's domesticity matched Smith's dreams. They adopted pet names: Smith was "Jeddy"; Green, "Liddy"; Cozens, "Heddy"; and Oakley preferred "Violet, Duchess of Oaks." So, in 1900, when the four—tired of cramped city apartments—learned that a picturesque estate was available for lease, they resolved to make it theirs, though the $125 monthly rent exceeded all of their city rents combined.

"The move to the Red Rose Inn necessitated a stronger, more binding commitment among all four women," writes historian Alice A. Carter. "So just before the move, they made...a solemn agreement to stay together for life."

The house provided large living and studio spaces, gardens and countryside, as well as personal and professional support. It was the perfect backdrop for Green's and Smith's romantic domestic images, as well as—oddly—for the historic scenes that became Oakley's specialty. Soon after moving in, Oakley won a commission to paint eighteen murals for the Governor's Reception Room at the new capitol. She chose the theme of religious freedom that led to the founding of Pennsylvania and left among her papers dozens of photographic studies of her friends posing in colonial costumes.

Smith had a variety of clients but increasingly focused on children. She illustrated exposés such as "While the Mother Works: A Look at the Day Nurseries of New York" (*Century* magazine, 1902), books such as *Scribners Child's Garden of Verses* and, later, produced dreamy, flattering portraits of the offspring of well-heeled private clients.

Meanwhile, Jeddy and Heddy were becoming increasingly devoted to each other; Smith wrote more intimately to Cozens than her ex-fiancé ever had. "The reading class was taken in the library and I wandered in thinking I would try and listen," Smith wrote to Cozens in 1906. "I soon realized I was not there at all. I was spending the evening in a dark flower-decked room where a very precious little person is with blue bows in her hair."

The Red Rose Inn days ended abruptly in 1906. The property had been sold, and the new owner wanted the women out. To those who pleaded on the Cogs' behalf, Henry Kerbaugh insisted, "I don't want any beggarly artists on the place!" Eventually, they found a house in Mount Airy and named it Cogslea.

Green and Oakley were younger, and the latter, in particular, had ambitions beyond aesthetics. Oakley, who had spent months in England researching the capitol paintings and became entranced with William Penn, could expound for hours about the Holy Experiment. Her work also showed a growing feminist streak, with strong female allegorical figures a trademark. A powerful female representing peace and freedom dominates a full third of her sixty-foot mural, *Unity*, in the Senate chamber. As World War I approached, Oakley hoped that the themes of her murals might help turn the country away from the conflict. Possibly, she didn't notice the growing friendship between Green and Huger Elliott.

Reporting on the wedding, the *Chestnut Hill Herald* said that Oakley had pleaded with Green to change her mind. When she did not, Oakley "broke down completely." Five years later, Oakley invited a student, Edith Emerson (1888–1981), to help in her studio. Emerson never left, serving as president of the Violet Oakley Memorial Foundation until her death in 1981. In 1914, after Oakley and Green went their separate ways, Smith and Cozens moved from Cogslea to a house they built for themselves. They named it Cogshill.

Nobody knows what happened in those bedrooms. So perhaps a friend of the Cogs summarized it best: "What does it matter if they were orgasmic? The point is they loved each other."

Politics aside, of course.

1902

A Trail to Nowhere

A mere 2.2 miles long, the stub of the defunct Philadelphia & Western Railroad that Radnor converted to a hiking and biking trail is barely enough to spike a serious biker's heart rate. It is literally a trail to nowhere.

But that was precisely the alibi that George Gould needed in 1902. Gould, son of cutthroat railroad financier Jay Gould, intended that his modest commuter line from Sixty-ninth Street to Strafford would crush the powerful Pennsylvania Railroad. Gould planned to link the P&W with other lines to reach Pittsburgh, there connecting with still other lines to the Pacific. The Pennsy, which didn't extend beyond Chicago, wouldn't be able to compete.

Gould's failure illustrates the hazards of trying to civilize capitalism. Had George been as cutthroat as old Jay, the Main Line might now be sitting on a very long bike trail indeed.

To Jay Gould (1836–1892), business was war. The son of a poor New York farmer, Gould chose a business career at age fourteen while hoeing corn. Gould hated hoeing corn. He also hated plowing, planting, shoveling manure, chasing and milking cows and everything else to do with farming. The village school offered no hope of escape.

So, Jay made a deal with his father: His brother would inherit the farm, freeing Jay to pursue a career in business. Or, more accurately, to pursue wealth. Gould was never much interested in what money could buy: his father owned property but labored hard. What Gould wanted was so much money that it would work for him.

A Philadelphia & Western trolley stops at its Sugartown Road Station—a site occupied in 2010 by a Wawa convenience store—shortly before the line was abandoned in 1955. *Radnor Historical Society.*

Gould's first job was with a surveyor mapping a neighboring county. When the surveyor went bankrupt, Gould offered to sell his "interest" in the project to his employers' creditors for $500—three times his wages. Next, he talked himself into a junior partnership in a tannery near Stroudsburg. Without informing the absentee senior partner, Zadoc Pratt, Gould poured all the profits into his own private investment. Then he used the money to speculate in other businesses. Pratt caught on and, in his disgust, allowed Gould to walk away with half of the tannery's value just to be rid of him. The poor farmer's son was now worth about $60,000.

So it went. In an unregulated era when business was conducted on faith and a handshake, Gould abused both. In 1867, while a director of the Erie Railroad, Gould conspired with two other directors to wrest control from majority stockholder, Cornelius Vanderbilt. The trio issued thousands of shares of additional stock to water down the value of Vanderbilt's holdings. When a warrant was issued for their arrest, they moved the Erie's

A Philadelphia & Western trolley approaches its Villanova station in 1940. Conceived as a coast-to-coast railroad by railroad robber baron Jay Gould, the P&W always struggled as a commuter line. *Radnor Historical Society.*

headquarters to Jersey City, beyond the reach of New York law. That gave Gould enough time to rush to Albany and pay off enough state legislators to win retroactive approval of the stock sale. The experience, said Vanderbilt, "learned me it never pays to kick a skunk."

The experience also launched Gould's love affair with railroads. Between 1872 and his death in 1892, Gould was a director of seventeen major railroad lines and president of five. He milked every one. In 1879, in his greatest personal coup, Gould blackmailed the Union Pacific Railroad into buying several parallel lines that he owned rather than face his competition. The maneuver netted Gould $10 million. He was president of the Union Pacific at the time.

Gould was not particularly bloodthirsty by the standards of his time, but his reputation was damaged by an aloof, arrogant personality. In 1886, dismissing a strike threat, he said, "I can hire one half the working class to kill the other half." Gould also refused to speak with reporters, who retaliated by savaging him. Finally, as Belle Waring, a great-great-granddaughter, recently observed, "He didn't go in for any of that pussy, reputation-burnishing charity either. Leave that to your guilt-ridden Carnegie and Rockefeller types."

As much as he loved railroad profits, Gould found rail travel inconvenient. In particular, it annoyed him that no railroad covered more than a third of the continent, which meant that cross-country travelers had to change trains several times. He dreamed of a single transcontinental system.

Gould died without realizing his dream, but he left his children an example to follow and a $77 million empire that included fifteen thousand miles of railroad track, extending from Detroit to Pueblo, Colorado. The task of extending the Gould system to the coasts fell to Jay's eldest son, George.

In the West, George Gould quietly bought up several short-line railroads to extend the family holdings to Utah and then launched construction of the Western Pacific from Salt Lake City to San Francisco. It was finished by 1909, despite harassment from the competing Union Pacific, which harassed Gould with snipers, sabotage and fomented strikes.

In the East—where the Pennsylvania Railroad was entrenched—Gould extended his Wabash Railroad from Toledo into Pittsburgh. Because the Pennsy had long staked out the natural routes into Pittsburgh, Gould was forced to bridge rivers and tunnel mountains. One tunnel was a mile long.

It cost millions but, according to historian Edwin P. Hoyt, Gould thought he had an ace in the hole: Andrew Carnegie, owner of U.S. Steel. Carnegie annually shipped about ten million tons to the East Coast, and in 1899, the Pennsy had doubled his rates.

"Carnegie professed to be infuriated, and perhaps he was," wrote Hoyt. "One could never tell with this shrewd old Scotsman who was capable, like Jay Gould, of pursuing several apparently contradictory schemes at once." If Carnegie switched his business to the new Gould line, the millions for construction would be well spent.

East of Pittsburgh, Gould planned to build to York, Pennsylvania, connecting with his newly purchased Western Maryland Railway, which ran from there to Baltimore. To reach Philadelphia and New York, he planned to build down the Main Line. At Sugartown Road, the track would be located only a few blocks from Pennsy's Strafford station.

George Gould's problem was that everyone knew what he was doing, something never said of his father. Jay Gould had learned to be secretive while scratching his way out of poverty, but George had been born to wealth. He didn't consider anyone a threat.

So, Gould's fingerprints were obvious when the P&W incorporated in 1902, with announced intentions to build only from Cobbs Creek at Sixty-third and Market Streets to Parkesburg forty-four miles away. The P&W was organized as a railroad—giving it the power of eminent domain and the right to connect to other railroads—and not as a trolley company. Unlike most trolleys, the P&W did not cross a single highway or railroad. In its first twelve-mile segment from Sixty-ninth Street to Strafford, it built thirty-four bridges, boosting construction costs to $400,000 per mile.

To allay suspicions, Gould first picked unknowns to head P&W. In 1905, however, William T. Van Brunt took over. Van Brunt was president of the St. Joseph and Grand Island Railroad, and his election as president of P&W made the line more suspicious. In July 1905, P&W found it necessary to issue a statement that "[n]one of the various railroads—the Pennsylvania, Wabash, Reading or Lehigh Valley—mentioned at various times as identified with the road are in any way interested, nor have they a dollar in the property."

Still, the Pennsy was nervous. Its president, Alexander Cassatt, announced that it would increase the number of tracks between Philadelphia and Paoli from four to six and add more trains.

Then, it all collapsed. Carnegie sold U.S. Steel to J.P. Morgan, an opponent of the Goulds who vowed never to ship steel over their lines. In 1907, a financial panic halved the value of the Gould railroads, which financed the expansion. Construction on the Western Pacific ran over budget by $25 million. To pay debts, George Gould had to give up the Wabash and the Western Maryland.

In 1906, in a last-gasp effort to attract capital, the P&W made what a Philadelphia newspaper called a "startling proposal." For a share of the profits, P&W asked Philadelphia to approve a subway line under Center City and the Delaware to New Jersey, where it would make connections for New York. Mayor John Weaver called it "a splendid proposal," but city council did not approve.

That left P&W to survive on its own, something it was never intended to do. Service began in October 1907 with trains running every fifteen minutes. But after the novelty wore off, ridership was meager. P&W netted only $19,500 on revenues of $350,000 in its first three years. Half of its cars sat unused.

The problem, according to railroad historian Ron DeGraw, was location. The P&W passed through only three significant towns: Ardmore, Bryn Mawr and Wayne. But it did so only on the edges, while Pennsy stations were located conveniently in the center of each business district.

"It became quite evident after only a couple of years of operation that the railroad could not survive as it was," wrote DeGraw. "It would have to go somewhere else."

Salvation came when investors bought the P&W and, in 1912, opened a connection between Radnor and the Lehigh Valley Transit Company (LVT) in North Wales. Previously, pokey little LVT trolleys had taken 3.5 hours to trundle from Allentown to Chestnut Hill, but service upgrades attracted new riders. A stump of this service survives today as Septa's Norristown line.

As for the Strafford branch, P&W tried many tricks to win riders, such as the reduced-fare packages to the Devon Horse Show. The company also investigated selling electricity from its powerhouses to nearby homeowners. Ridership surged briefly during World War II but melted away in the 1950s. The Strafford line was abandoned in 1955—all because George Gould didn't have his father's knack for shivving an opponent.

But wouldn't the Pennsy have made a great bike trail?

1910

GOOD AND FAITHFUL SERVANT

Poets are dangerous people. They write what they feel, not what someone pays or authorizes them to write. Poets set people free and—a bureaucrat might say—on the road to ruin. And, really, aren't we all bureaucrats?

In 1961, after Russian poet Yevgeny Yevtushenko published "Babi Yar" denouncing Soviet anti-Semitism, Communist bureaucrats concluded that he was the most dangerous man in the USSR and banned him from foreign travel. In the 1950s, southern sheriffs, newspapers and the Ku Klux Klan—the bureaucrats of segregation—chased poet-activist Don West out of Georgia for poems revealing the miseries of factory workers, sharecroppers and African Americans.

Which brings us to Bryn Mawr poet Elinor Wylie (1885–1928) who, as a student at the Baldwin School, first encountered the English Romantic poet Percy Bysshe Shelley (1792–1822). Shelley, who had denigrated religion and monarchy and celebrated individual happiness, emotions and spontaneity, abandoned his pregnant wife and child in 1814 to run away with another woman. A century later, in 1910, Wylie followed his example. After five years of a difficult marriage, she ditched husband and three-year-old son for a married man. In all, Wylie went through three husbands and several affairs.

"Most women instinctively sensed that, like Byron, she was 'mad, bad, and dangerous to know,' particularly if they had husbands at risk," wrote Wylie biographer Stanley Olson. "Elinor had a fatal effect on many of the lives she touched. She left behind her a wake of suicides, misadventures and tragedy."

Both Philip Hichborn, the first husband she deserted, and their son died by their own hands.

At Bryn Mawr's Baldwin School, the future poet Elinor Wylie discovered Shelley's 1816 "To a Skylark," which celebrated following one's muse. Wylie did exactly that, creating a reputation as one "mad, bad and dangerous to know." *Lower Merion Historical Society.*

Yet Wylie was considered a foremost poet of the 1920s. She also painted and wrote eight novels, but her poetry—based in emotional and intellectual contradiction—caught the disillusioned mood that followed World War I. Wylie wrote with a tone suggesting that she'd been lied to for a reading public that knew it had. Her 1921 poem "The Eagle and the Mole," for instance, was a clear call to shun what was popularly believed: "Avoid the reeking herd / Shun the polluted flock / Live like that stoic bird / The eagle of the rock / The huddled warmth of crowds / Begets and fosters hate / He keeps above the clouds / His cliff inviolate."

Born in Somerville, New Jersey, Elinor Morton Hoyt was the granddaughter of prominent Philadelphians who used their influence and money to draw the young family back to Rittenhouse Square and the Main Line by the time the child was two. The family alternated between a townhouse on Locust Street and a house on Lancaster Avenue in Rosemont. Her paternal grandfather, Henry Martyn Hoyt, had been a colonel in the Civil War and had served one term (1879–1883) as governor of Pennsylvania. Her maternal grandfather, Morton McMichael, had been editor of the *Saturday Evening Post* before serving as mayor of Philadelphia and, later, ambassador to Great Britain.

Elinor's father, also Henry Martyn Hoyt, was a lawyer who would serve as U.S. solicitor general during the Theodore Roosevelt and Taft administrations.

Elinor's mother, Anne McMichael, was a domineering parent who chose her children's playmates by the Social Register while using her chronic ill health—carefully maintained for sixty years—to control her family.

At Baldwin, Elinor followed an unusual curriculum designed to prepare students for admission to Bryn Mawr College: arithmetic, geometry, geography, observation and gymnastics. Her parents disapproved of higher education for women but chose Baldwin for its general excellence, especially its emphasis on literature.

"[Mama] held the belief...that 'schools and colleges are the last places to send girls,'" wrote Olson, "for the primary reason that they leave out training in goodness in the old religious sense."

Alas, Elinor also discovered Shelley's "To a Skylark," the 1816 poem in which he uses the bird as a metaphor for poetic inspiration: "hail to thee, blithe spirit! / Bird thou never wert." Like Shelley, this poet would follow her muses where they led.

In 1897, to Elinor's distress, her father was appointed an assistant attorney general by President McKinley, thus requiring a move to Washington. On "K" Street, however, the Hoyts continued to live in their upper-crust Philadelphia way. In the winter, there were formal balls and receptions; in summer, long visits to grandparents in Devon, idyllic months in Bar Harbor, Maine, and grand tours of Europe.

In 1903, after finishing classes at the Academy of Fine Arts—where she spent hours looking at the work of John Singer Sargent—Elinor made her social debut, which meant she was available for marriage. This interested her little, but neither was she interested in higher education. A career was out of the question.

"As the eldest of three daughters, the pressure to get married was fierce," wrote Olson. "Spinsterhood was an embarrassing state and the family had two unmarried aunts who brought no credit to the Hoyts. Elinor was virtually shoved at men."

She was a beautiful young woman and she did have admirers. But she wasn't really interested in men, except to satisfy her mother. After one awkward courtship that ended badly, Elinor was so embarrassed by her continuing singleness that she said "yes" to another young fellow who had been pestering her unsuccessfully for a year. They were married in 1906 in a small wedding at the Hoyt mansion. President Roosevelt was among the guests.

Philip Hichborn was a lawyer, but not a successful one. His greatest accomplishment was being charming. He was passionate about riding horses and hunting, played tennis well and was an excellent dancer. In the social circles in which he and Elinor moved, this counted for a lot. But there was also an unattractive side to his character. Hichborn was enormously jealous, often to the point of tantrums.

"These unmanageable outbursts of temper destroyed any relationship they might have shared," wrote Olson.

Elinor Hoyt Hichborn bore a child in 1907, after only ten months of marriage. But her husband was jealous of the attention she gave the infant, so being parents didn't bring them closer. Miserable, Elinor confided in her parents. Her mother, concerned first about appearances, urged her to suck it up. ("There is such a thing," she wrote, "as being too bad to be true.") Her father was prepared to help Elinor negotiate a divorce.

Meanwhile, she met Horace Wylie, who was seventeen years her senior. Like Phil Hichborn, he was a half-hearted lawyer who preferred to spend his time on gentlemanly pastimes—golf, hunting and bridge. He also relished the ungentlemanly game of chasing women.

"Horace Wylie," wrote Olson, "suffered from an intemperate weakness for beautiful women all his life." And he thought Elinor was beautiful, describing her as "the most beautiful person I had ever seen. I almost gasped" upon first seeing her.

In Elinor's domesticated world, she was seldom alone. But Wylie was shameless and persistent. One day, he made up a story about needing to check out the references of a furnace repairman to call on her. Elinor's mother-in-law was in the next room, so between Wylie's loud queries about the functioning of her heating system he whispered his real mission. He recited, "at considerable length," wrote Olson, the charms of her hair and wrists. There were accidental meetings in theatres and on the sidewalk that weren't accidental at all. Eventually, in Washington's Rock Creek Park, they kissed in Wylie's automobile.

The 1910 death of Henry Hoyt may have been the turning point. Her father's sympathy for her marital misery, Elinor discovered, had been rooted in his own. He'd had a mistress for years, possibly a secretary at the Department of Justice. The woman had come to the house only once—to say goodbye, as Hoyt lay dying—but Elinor's mother refused to let her in. The younger woman determined not to let her own life pass in the same way.

Horace wrote a letter to his wife; Elinor, to her husband. In Atlantic City, her mother received a letter from Elinor that read, "Don't let this kill you…I have run away," and fainted.

Elinor's brother and husband searched ships in New York, but the couple had taken a train to Canada and then a ship to Europe. And there, in the face of lurid newspaper stories and despite entreaties from both families, they remained—under assumed names in a cottage in England. They only returned to the United States at the outbreak of World War I, when the British government insisted that aliens leave the country. In 1916, after extensively reported divorces, they finally married, and Elinor Hoyt Hichborn assumed what would be her pen name, Elinor Wylie. They returned to Washington in 1919, and Wylie found herself moving in literary circles.

Wylie had always written, but her new friends—among them the writer John Dos Passos and the critic Edmund Wilson—convinced her to pursue writing seriously. *Poetry* magazine published four poems in 1920, which was followed by her first book, *Nets to the Wind*, the following year. That same year, Wylie left her second husband and moved to New York. The difference in their ages had finally caused them to drift apart. They later divorced.

There followed three more volumes of verse and four novels, several of which won high praise from America's most influential critics. Her notoriety did not hurt sales. One critic, William Rose Benét, became Wylie's third husband in 1923. They separated in 1926 but remained married and occasionally lived together. During the last year of her life, she became romantically involved with Henry de Clifford Woodhouse, the husband of a friend. The relationship inspired the love sonnets in her last book, *Angels and Earthly Creatures*. She finished the final draft one night in December 1928 and then died of a stroke.

Wylie was buried with a laurel wreath around her head, placed by another poet, Edna St. Vincent Millay, who had a similarly interesting personal life. The verse on her tombstone—"Well done, thou good and faithful servant"—was from Shelley and undoubtedly referred to her poetry.

Scene from a Marriage

Some women really can't be satisfied. As Exhibit A, consider Lucile Polk Carter (1875–1934) of Bryn Mawr, whose husband got her and their two children safely into a lifeboat when the *Titanic* was sinking beneath them in 1912.

Grateful? Not much. Lucile subsequently divorced William E. Carter (1875–1940), whose crime seems to have been that he survived, too.

Carter was the grandson of coal baron William T. Carter, who opened a mine in Luzerne County during the Civil War and got so rich on anthracite that his bedroom furniture is now in the Pennsylvania Museum of Art. But the younger Carter spent little time in the mines. Before boarding the *Titanic* on April 10, the Carters had spent the winter in England's Melton Mowbray district, a traditional center of fox hunting and high society. A "sportsman" who spent most of his time chasing foxes and playing polo, Carter was a regular at the Germantown and Merion cricket clubs and a familiar face in Newport, Rhode Island, where the social elite spent its summers.

Lucile was part of a Baltimore family who had also produced James K. Polk, the eleventh president of the United States. She and Carter married in 1897 and lived at Bryn Mawr in a mansion named Gwenda, where a daughter and son were born in 1898 and 1900, respectively, and named for their parents (i.e., Lucile and William Jr.).

Carter was also taking home a new twenty-five-horsepower French Renault automobile, which was disassembled, crated and loaded in *Titanic*'s hold. In a 1997 movie, the Renault was shown fully assembled so that stars

In 1912, aboard the rescue ship *Carpathia*, William Carter of Bryn Mawr called down to his wife in a *Titanic* lifeboat like this that he'd had "a jolly good breakfast and was never sure she would make it." She divorced him. *Library of Congress.*

Kate Winslet and Leonardo DiCaprio could steam up its windows. Also along for the ride were Carter's polo ponies and the family servants: Auguste Serreplan, her maid; Alexander Cairns, his manservant; and Charles Aldworth, the chauffeur.

They did not lack company. When the *Titanic* steamed west, it carried some of the Carters' closest acquaintances. Among them were John B. Thayer, forty-nine, of Haverford, a vice-president of the Pennsylvania Railroad, and George D. Widener, fifty, of Elkins Park, heir to probably the largest fortune in Philadelphia and a member of the board of Fidelity Trust bank. (Fidelity controlled International Mercantile Marine, which owned the White Star Line and, in turn, *Titanic*.) Thayer, his wife and their son Jack had spent the previous two weeks as guests of the U.S. consul general in Berlin. The Wideners—George, his wife Eleanor and their son Harry—had been guests at the Ritz Hotel in Paris, which Harry, a twenty-seven-year-old book collector, had scoured for rare volumes.

On the afternoon of April 14, George Widener and his wife were seen standing on the promenade deck talking with J. Bruce Ismay, managing director of White Star, when Captain Edward Smith passed on his way aft. Without comment, Smith handed Ismay a fresh message from the liner *Baltic*, warning of ice ahead. Ismay put the message in his pocket.

That evening, in Captain Smith's honor, the Wideners hosted a dinner party also attended by the Thayers, the Carters and Major Archibald Butt, a military adviser to President Theodore Roosevelt. Shortly before 9:00 p.m., Smith excused himself and headed for the bridge. After the women retired, the men sat in the smoking room to talk. "No one had any thought of danger," Carter told the *Washington Times* five days later.

The men were still talking at 11:40 p.m. when the ship struck the iceberg. After assessing the situation, Carter walked to his family's cabins, B96 and B98, where accounts diverge.

Carter later claimed that he told his wife to wake the children, dress warmly and accompany him to the lifeboat stations. What Lucile later said in her divorce application was this: "When the *Titanic* struck, my husband came to our stateroom and said, 'Get up and dress yourself and the children.' I never saw him again until I arrived at the *Carpathia* at 8 o'clock the next morning, when I saw him leaning on the rail."

Most accounts of the sinking agree that *Titanic* passengers were initially reluctant to enter lifeboats. It was warm and bright and dry in the cabins and cold and dark and wet out on the sea. So, even though Lucile and the children were probably dressed and topside by midnight or so, they and other passengers dawdled, ignoring the crew's urgings as minutes ticked away. Lifeboat no. 4, with Lucile and the two children aboard, did not finally depart *Titanic* until 1:55 a.m. *Titanic* sank at 2:20 a.m.

Carter was probably unaware of this. Lifeboat no. 4 was on the port side of the ship, and the crew loading it—to facilitate the "women and children first" rule—had ordered all men to the starboard side. Having delivered his family to the lifeboats, Carter had no choice but to seek safety on his own. In such a situation, what does one do?

Carter did what society folks usually do. He huddled with his friends to talk it over. Fortunes are not made or kept by acting rashly. He asked Harry Widener whether the young book-lover was going to try for a lifeboat.

Widener dismissed the notion. "I think I'll stick to the big ship, Billy, and take a chance," is how Carter later quoted him. The story conflicts with a legend among *Titanic* buffs that Harry missed a lifeboat when he ran to his cabin to retrieve a rare 1598 copy of *Bacon's Essays*.

By about 2:00 a.m., all of the regular lifeboats were gone. Carter was watching the crew unlash and load women into two collapsible lifeboats. (*Titanic* had four collapsibles, which had wood bottoms and canvas sides that "collapsed" to allow them to be stored in little space.) Order was breaking down: a crowd of desperate men tried to push their way into Collapsible C, and two dining room stewards actually jumped in from a deck above. At this point, Purser Herbert McElroy fired his pistol in the air. The crowd drew back. The stewards were thrown out. Loading continued until there were no more women and children in the vicinity. As the boat was released for lowering, Carter and another man stepped in. The other man was Ismay.

To many—and, it seems, particularly to Lucile—it was all rather shameful. First, there was the problem that Carter survived at all. In 1912, male gallantry was widely valued. The proof is in the statistics: only 18 percent of adult male passengers survived versus 72 percent of female passengers. When Eleanor Widener and Marian Thayer arrived home as widows, they had the comfort of friends who admired their men's valor. Not Lucile.

"William's big mistake was ending up as a live husband rather than a dead hero," said *Titanic* scholar Robert Godfrey. "This didn't go down well in the social circles that Lucile moved in."

Men who survived for "legitimate" reasons suffered no stigma. Richard Norris Williams of Wayne, a national tennis champion, was thrown in the water and was washed toward a lifeboat by the splash of a falling stack.

Further muddying Carter's name was the fact that his manservant and chauffeur both died, even though—by the standards of noblesse oblige—he was responsible for their well-being.

Another problem was Ismay. Despite his denials, rumors had it that Ismay urged Smith to ignore ice warnings in the hope of setting a speed record. That would have made Ismay responsible for the wreck and his survival particularly shameful.

"The general feeling seemed to be," wrote historian Logan Marshall, "that he should have stayed aboard the sinking vessel, looking out for those who were left, playing the man like Major Butt and many another and going down with the ship like Captain Smith." Carter, who stepped into the lifeboat with Ismay and backed up his story, suffered from the association.

Another problem: *Carpathia* picked up Carter first. So he was safe aboard the rescue ship when Lifeboat no. 4 carrying Lucile and the children was brought alongside. Then he had the bad taste to lean over the railing and say to his wife—in his jocular, clubhouse way—that he'd had "a jolly good breakfast and was never sure she would make it."

Complicating things further was that Lucile behaved well by the standards of the time. She'd pulled an oar. She'd not gotten hysterical. For a man, this would have been nothing much. For a woman, it was enough for the papers to call her a heroine.

Combined, it all made William Carter look like a coward. The condescension was apparent when the *New York Times* dryly reported that the Carters, "the only Philadelphia family on the *Titanic* to be rescued without the loss of a member, show few effects of their experience."

Lucile endured the snubbing for eighteen months and then filed for divorce. Her accusations regarding the sinking were sealed by the court but leaked to the press, causing a sensation. She remarried four months after the final decree and went to live near Pottstown.

Carter seems to have carried the stigma for the rest of his life. He never remarried and spent much of his time at his country house, Gwenda Farm, near Unionville, where neighbors called him "Titanic Bill" behind his back.

Considering the high price of pleasing the public and Lucile, though, perhaps the stigma was worth it.

1921

LOVE OF LEARNING

E ducation gives people ideas. But if education costs an arm and a leg, are ideas something fewer people can afford?

Today, financial advisers discourage majors that don't command high premiums in the job market. Top choices, then, are accounting, engineering and business. English? Drama? Not so much. Yet the liberal arts were top choices at a free summer school for working-class women at Bryn Mawr College in the early twentieth century.

From 1921 to 1938, the college partnered with the YWCA and, informally, with several trade unions. The Bryn Mawr Summer School for Women Workers annually brought to campus one hundred tradeswomen, most in their twenties, for eight weeks of classes in economics, English, history, literature, hygiene, science and the appreciation of music. Costs were paid by donors, including the Carnegie Foundation, John D. Rockefeller and Mrs. Pierre DuPont.

It ended when the women demonstrated an unseemly ability to think for themselves, even though that had been the school's avowed purpose.

"We were not just nice girls anymore," said the late Ester Peterson (1906–1997), director of dramatics and recreation. "We were vigorous people who wanted to change society."

The idea belonged to Bryn Mawr president M. Carey Thomas (1857–1935), who returned from a 1920 tour of North Africa with a revelation. The Nineteenth Amendment granting women the right to vote—which Thomas supported—had been ratified. Later, in her typical purplish prose, Thomas described the moment:

One afternoon at sunset I was sitting on a golden hilltop, in the [Sahara] desert, rejoicing that British women had just been enfranchised, realizing that American women would soon be politically free and wondering what would be the next great social advance. Suddenly, as in a vision, I seemed to see…that the coming of equal opportunity for the manual workers of the world might be hastened by utilizing the deep sympathy that women now feel for one another.

Raising their working-class sisters was an issue of gender solidarity. The tool she proposed was a version of worker schools already common in England.

"There is no reason why the same thing should not be done in the United States," Thomas remarked. "Every summer there are empty college buildings all over the country."

This was a big personal advance for Thomas, who had long believed that society should be ruled by its "best" people—the educated, the wealthy and those who appreciated culture. Now, she seemed to realize, that was not enough. The best must share their values with the rest.

To manage the school, Thomas chose Hilda Worthington Smith as college dean. Smith—known on campus as "Jane"—was known for helping people bridge differences. In 1910, as student body president, she had helped convince two rival student religious groups—one theologically conservative, the other liberal—to merge into a new moderate association. For Smith, the summer school was a piece of good timing: with the recent death of her mother, she felt in a rut.

"But I was stirred in spite of myself by the discussions of the proposed school," she wrote in an unpublished autobiography.

Smith built a network of alumnae, churches, labor unions and benefactors to set policy and recruit students. The board aimed for diversity in religion, the industries in which the women worked and, eventually, race. Half would be union members, which in that era was bound to bring in some Reds. Smith placed the share of communists at 8 percent.

"There was no secrecy about it," she said in a 1969 interview. "And they were very stimulating in the school."

This had its lighter moments. When students and faculty played off-hours baseball, one woman performed water carrier duties with a hammer and sickle pinned to her shirt. Those she considered capitalists had to beg for water.

Requirements for admission included an elementary education and two years of nonsupervisory experience in any industry. Advantages were maturity, leadership skills, curiosity and awareness of economic issues.

At the first eight-week session, there were New York garment workers, a Philadelphia milliner who came with her mother, textile workers from New England, telephone operators from Cincinnati and a waitress from Colorado. Polish, Czech, Lithuanian, Irish and Scottish immigrants mixed with southern whites who had never met a foreigner. "An Italian dressmaker," wrote Smith, "rejoiced to find other Italian girls and hurried off to telegraph her mother of this reassuring discovery." Most arrived by train, but a group of Russians hitchhiked.

"Girls from the same city were never put together," wrote Smith. "Friends were ruthlessly separated." Co-religionists and unionists roomed together. The intent was to give everyone new contacts but avoid explosive differences.

The school immediately faced two challenges. First, many students were terrified. Typically, Bryn Mawr women believed higher education to be their right. These women did not.

"Many were afraid they would not be equal to the task," wrote Smith. "They were afraid of the teachers, and even afraid to change chairs in the cafeteria." One asked permission to walk from one dorm to another. To Smith, this was proof that—in addition to "breaking her body and warping her mind"—the factory system broke a woman's spirit.

"With no voice in the affairs of her own industry," she wrote, "with fear inbred in all her relations with boss or foreman, she had become dependent on others to tell her what to do and dared not act for herself in new situations." (This changed.)

Second, many union women were suspicious. "[Union officials] said it was capitalistic," wrote Smith, "and that they would only be propagandized." It didn't help that many arrived through an arch of Rockefeller Hall, the 1904 gift of the strikebreaking founder of Standard Oil.

"Does Mr. Rockefeller run this school?" asked one.

Long discussions followed about "tainted money," said student Freddy Drake Payne in *Women of Summer*, a 1986 film about the school. "Ultimately," she said, "we decided it was more important where the money went than where it came from." To win over skeptics, the college also gave students half the board seats. Thomas at first opposed this, believing educators should be in charge.

"Jane [Smith] had the wit and wisdom to bring some of the students to a luncheon that Thomas was having and gave her a chance to hear from them," said student Carmen Lucia, who later became an organizer for the hatter's union. "She changed her mind."

For Lucia, that was a life lesson. "History didn't just happen to you," she said. "It was up to you to change it."

The school granted no degrees, so classroom methods could be unconventional: drama and role playing, debates and discussion. But instruction was also purposeful. Smith believed that students should build on their work experience to understand larger issues and develop a sense of responsibility for solutions.

Smith later recalled an exercise in which a New England textile worker graphed changes in her wages, her hours and the number of her looms over a five-year period. Her hours had gone up, it seemed, and her wages down, while the number of her looms had increased each year. "She looked at the finished chart intently," wrote Smith, "and remarked, 'I knew something had been happening to me, but I never realized just what it was before.'"

Surviving interviews suggest that the school described to donors was different from its reality. Its charter mandated impartial, nondogmatic inquiry. But faculty economist Broadus Mitchell admitted that "advancing the rights and influence of organized labor infused all instruction."

Mitchell was more radical than some students. When he condemned the "cruelty" of repetitive labor, for instance, one woman disagreed. "She said she used the time for contemplation," said Mitchell. The pro-labor bias intensified with the Depression.

In 1936, after the U.S. Supreme Court ruled unconstitutional several parts of the National Industrial Recovery Act, students produced a theatrical satire in which factory workers tried to make small improvements in their conditions. At crucial junctures, a group of judges would rise and chant, "Null and void, null and void, unconstitutional, unconstitutional." Peterson praised its "freshness."

Yet students tempered themselves when necessary. Guest lecturers included birth control advocate Margaret Sanger, civil rights activist W.E.B. DuBois, socialist Norman Thomas and labor leader Walter Reuther. But when the students invited one particularly radical speaker—whom Smith did not name—they paused.

"A leading communist student came to my room at midnight and asked if having the speaker would really hurt the school," wrote Smith, who predicted a crisis but promised not to interfere. The students voted to un-invite the speaker.

"They came to care for the school," wrote Smith, "and because they came to care about it, they always modified their recommendations, rather entirely on their own initiative."

Some "modified" less. When anarchists Sacco and Vanzetti were executed in 1927, summer school people joined a Center City protest. A professor was arrested, generating a newspaper headline: "Bryn Mawr: A Hotbed of Radicalism." Greater and lesser incidents followed.

The final straw came in 1936 when students and faculty observed (or took part in; accounts vary) a strike against Seabrook Farms in New Jersey. In 1934, Seabrook extended and then withdrew recognition of its agricultural workers' union. Picketing went on for years. Peterson went and considered the experience educational.

"You have to see it and smell it and hear it to understand," she said. "These things don't arise just because there is propaganda. They arise because there is a sore."

There was violence. Rocks were thrown. Fire hoses were used on strikers and their families, including pregnant women. Again, the school was in the papers, and this time, its supporters decided to withdraw.

"The corporations that had helped us said, 'Why should we give money when you're training people to come and organize my plant?'" said Peterson.

The school dissolved after its 1938 session. Still, everyone got quite an education.

1928

SHOPPING THE
GENERATIONS

Suburban Square has been a fixture on the lower Main Line since 1928, so it's easy to forget how revolutionary it once was—and, in some ways, is again.

To appreciate Suburban Square's significance, let's consider the men who built it: developers Ledyard Heckscher, James K. Stone and Francis Von A. Cabeen. All were born in the 1870s and, therefore, were members of what social analysts William Strauss and Neil Howe called the "Missionary Generation."

According to Strauss and Howe, generational identity did not begin with the World War II generation and their troublesome, counterculture baby boomer kids. They described a pattern of four generational types—prophets, nomads, heroes and artists—that repeat through history.

"Appreciating the rhythm of this drama will enable you to foresee much of what the future holds for your own lifecycle," they wrote, "as well as what it holds for your children or grandchildren."

Now mostly forgotten, Missionaries were a prophet generation: values-driven, moralistic, focused on self and willing to fight for what they believed. They were the indulged children of the affluent post–Civil War era and, later, the grandparents of the generation who fought World War II. Born 1860–82, Missionaries came of age as fierce critics of the world that their veteran fathers had created—"a world," said Missionary writer George Cabot Lodge, "of machine guns and machine-everything-else."

Reform was their motto. Members of this generation included preachy student leaders, rebellious career women and Haymarket rioters. Upton

Ardmore's Suburban Square was built by a generation who saw shopping as a cultural and leisure activity and then nearly ruined by the utilitarian "greatest generation." Rescued and revived by baby boomers, it is again in transition. *Lower Merion Historical Society.*

Sinclair (1878–1968) sparked reform of the meatpacking industry with his novel *The Jungle*; birth-control advocate Margaret Sanger (1879–1966) started a revolution in the role of women that is still felt; and W.E.B. DuBois (1868–1963) was a spokesman for a rising generation of African Americans tired of Jim Crow. Both women's suffrage and Prohibition were enacted on the Missionaries' watch.

If this sounds familiar, it's because the baby boomers are also a prophet generation.

Missionaries hated what they considered the overly ornamented lives of their Victorian parents. In architecture, they abandoned gingerbread for the clean lines and simple shapes of Missionary architect Frank Lloyd Wright. Disdaining carved scrollwork, their Mission-style furniture featured "simple, honest" craftsmanship assembled with visible pegs.

In the Delaware Valley, Missionaries created Arden, a commune where artists and craftsmen turned out honest, hand-made objects and where all property was held in common.

From this perspective, Suburban Square can be seen as a Missionary shopping utopia. Like Arden, it was removed from the big, dirty city. Like other utopias, it was the result of "a soundly conceived and practical plan," not haphazard development. Some applicants, the developers proudly noted, were turned away "because they did not fit into the picture which the owners had envisioned." Early promotional literature described Suburban Square as an "experiment" that—combined with the automobile—offered a solution to the problem of congested cities.

"[Customers] motor in from all over the Main Line," proclaimed a 1930 brochure. "They park their cars comfortably near the shops they wish to patronize; their packages are deposited in their cars by polite attendants. Thus, they avoid the delays of deliveries from the city. And they have never a worry about a 'ticket' summoning them to a traffic court."

The promoters even gushed about Suburban Square's new gas station—a Sunoco—with "ample room on all sides [that] make it easily accessible." It was located at Montgomery and Anderson Avenues in the space occupied in 2010 by a Banana Republic store.

Planning for the center began in 1926 when Stone and his partners bought Thorncroft, an 1881 mansion on six acres. The center opened in 1928, despite opposition from Lancaster Avenue business owners fearing competition from regional chain stores and from homeowners fearing traffic and noise.

Unlike downtown Philadelphia, which then offered even less parking than it does now, Suburban Square offered angled parking right in front of its stores. Only the rich owned cars, so this perk was aimed straight at the Main Line gentry. The masses, it was believed, would arrive via a Lancaster Avenue trolley or the Pennsylvania Railroad's commuter line. The anticipated result: accessible shopping without congestion.

To design their dream, Stone and his partners chose a young local architect, Frederick W. Dreher. Dreher was not a Missionary but was instead part of the so-called Lost Generation, a Gen X–like nomad group: "ratty, tough, unwanted, diverse, adventurous and cynical about institutions." Again and again, the Missionaries turned to the Lost to execute their ideas.

Born 1883–1900, the Lost were the foot soldiers of World War I. Missionaries proclaimed the war a "Crusade for Democracy," but when it achieved only a frustrating armistice, the Lost were unfairly tagged as losers. Because they were younger, the Lost became the main targets of Missionary efforts to purge the country of liquor through the Volstead Act and vice through the Palmer Raids. The Lost also suffered most from the Depression, losing what should have been their peak earning years.

All buildings were constructed of the same creamy limestone with restrained Art Deco detailing, and the developers made much of Suburban Square's "modern" and "homogenous" architecture. Diversity was not something that the Missionaries much valued; their passion was to do things correctly. The architectural hodgepodge of Center City was not for them, nor the compromises required when existing buildings are adapted to retail. Suburban Square buildings, they stressed, were "in all cases especially designed for lessees."

Making peace with the community took a while. Financially, Suburban Square was such a success that Strawbridge & Clothier decided almost immediately to expand. That further unnerved the community, which in 1932 began talking about expanding Lower Merion's bare-bones zoning ordinance into a full-fledged development plan. To ensure that its voice was heard, the developers' Suburban Company launched its own daily newspaper. It survives today as a weekly, the *Main Line Times*.

Some things didn't go as planned. Neither the developers nor their architect anticipated a future in which most people drove cars. By the late 1970s, according to one study, up to two thousand cars per hour were competing for one of forty metered spaces near Strawbridge's.

Then there were the plebian tastes of the younger generations. The developers had presumed that most shoppers would have their purchases delivered. (Among the affluent, being seen carrying a package was a faux pas.) When Strawbridge's opened in 1930, it intended merely to show samples of merchandise that could be ordered from the downtown store. After discovering that this wouldn't do, the retailer expanded to carry merchandise in depth.

By mid-century, housing and subdivisions were beginning to fill the map, and Suburban Square was becoming just another place to buy stuff. A nice place, to be sure, but not the utopia its Missionary builders had had in mind.

Alongside what a local journalist described as the "hushed marble halls" of Strawbridge's sprang up smaller merchants selling practical things such as cameras, bed linens, plants, gardening tools and TV sets. In the 1950s, there was even a paint store.

What had happened was the arrival of the GI generation, a "hero" generation that emphasized the importance of getting things done and not *how* they were done. Delighted just to have survived the war, these then twenty- and thirtysomethings were further thrilled to be able to buy homes and cars. For them, savoring the quality of the shopping experience was irrelevant.

"We don't have shoppers anymore," said one merchant during these years. "We only have buyers."

By the late 1970s, this approach was wearing thin. Sales were stagnant. Retail action had shifted to newer centers such as the King of Prussia Mall. And with a new prophet generation (the baby boomers) starting to earn serious money, the center's owners had to get their attention. They started by sweeping out its dull GI accumulation.

First went the cars. Parking was offered on peripheral lots, but St. George's Road running through the heart of the center became a pedestrian mall. Then it was planted with trees and benches that encouraged shoppers to linger. The GIs, alas, had never learned to linger.

Many longtime shoppers complained about no longer being able to park in front the stores. And David Endy, owner of Seidenburg Luggage (and a GI), remembered being stunned that the trees cost $1,000 apiece. (Eventually, he grew to consider them "magnificent.")

A subsequent updating in the 1990s brought still lusher landscaping and a bubbling fountain worthy of any Italian piazza. "This center was not pretty," said baby boomer Kathy Sawin, the center's vice-president for leasing in the mid-1990s. "No plants, no flowers, not a green leaf before we took over."

Next went the boring stores—a lamp store, a wallpaper store, a fabric store and a sporting goods store so old-fashioned it sold sweats and tennis balls. Even F.A.O. Schwartz got bounced. (Having not yet reinvented itself as an upper-end toy "experience," Schwartz was losing sales to the likes of Kiddie City. After its makeover, the chain would have been welcome, a manager later said.)

In their place came waves of trendier stores selling things that were, perhaps, less useful but more fun. Out went the white foundation garments sold discreetly by Strawbridge's back in the '50s; in came brightly colored (and prominently displayed) stripper wear from Victoria's Secret. Out went the chaste pearl necklaces that defunct Diesinger's Jeweler's once suggested men buy for their wives and girlfriends; in came Caldwell Jeweler's chunky David Yurman bracelets that career women were buying for themselves.

Williamsburg reproduction furniture was out; Mission-style furniture from Restoration Hardware was in. Fresh flowers from Klinghoffer's replaced plants for the yard at Garden Mart.

The A&P that so impressed Main Liners in the '30s has been out for a long time. In its place at the turn of the twenty-first century was an expanded Ardmore Farmer's Market with the likes of Ardmore Seafood, Genji Sushi Express, Bucks County Coffee, Stoltzfus Poultry and many others.

Like the Missionaries, the baby boomers' version of Suburban Square had a plan. By banning cars, it has regained some of the serenity it had when cars were rare. By opting for merchants with the power to wow, it restored the sort of shopping experience that brought shoppers flocking through the Depression.

But nothing lasts forever. The center's core audience is women age twenty-five to fifty-four, now mostly Gen-Xers and Millennials (scheduled to be another "hero" generation.) Ten years into the new century, many of the baby boomers' stores—Caldwell's, Restoration Hardware and Klinghoffer's—are now gone. The center used Facebook and other Internet "social media" sites to reach shoppers. The Square had also acquired a very practical Pearle Vision store, plus an Apricot Lane shop whose line of "affordable" jewelry for women age thirteen to twenty-four was just right for Great Recession shoppers. And, somehow, Apple Computer, riding a wave of popularity among twenty-somethings, talked management into permitting a trendy metallic façade over its limestone exterior.

So wait around. Eventually, you may again be able to park in front of Strawbridge's (or, as it is temporarily known, Macy's).

1938
RUFUS TALKS WITH CREEPS

Does speaking with creeps encourage them? Political leaders think so. Washington, for instance, hasn't officially spoken with the government of Cuba since 1960 and of Iran since 1980. Eventually, this is supposed to make those governments less creepy.

Rufus Jones (1863–1948), Haverford College professor and co-founder of the American Friends Service Committee (AFSC), had a more-is-better theory about talk. In 1938, as governments recalled ambassadors to protest the Nazi *Kristallnacht* ("Night of Broken Glass") rampage against Jews, Jones didn't think himself too good to speak with the premier creeps of the twentieth century. Instead, Jones and two colleagues went to Berlin to intercede for the persecuted.

"We do not come to judge or criticize or to push ourselves in," the Quakers assured Gestapo chief Reinhard Heydrich (1904–1942), the primary architect of the Final Solution, "but to inquire in the most friendly manner whether there is anything we can do to promote life and human welfare and to relieve suffering."

It worked briefly. AFSC's Berlin office subsequently reported "a new freedom in making arrangements for Jewish families and in bringing relief. This short reprieve meant the difference between life and death to some families."

Born in South China, Maine, Jones was delivered by the village doctor into the arms of his aunt, Peace Jones, who predicted, "This child will one day bear the message of the Gospel to distant lands and to peoples across the sea."

Quaker Rufus Jones, retired Haverford College professor, went to Berlin in 1938 to plead for the Jews in the office of Reinhard Heydrich, primary architect of the Final Solution. It was crazy and naïve and, briefly, worked. *American Friends Service Committee.*

Not wealthy, the family was self-sustaining and religious in the Quaker way. When small, Rufus told his father that something "hurt like the devil," to which Edwin Jones responded slowly: "Thee is never to use that expression again in thy whole life." (Adult Rufus claimed he hadn't.) Attending worship twice weekly despite ample chores, Jones's parents impressed on him the importance of regular communion with God. "I was not 'christened' in a church," he wrote, "but I was sprinkled from morning to night with the dew of religion."

The family had a Bible and compensated for the scarcity of other books with visitors. Rufus grew up in an era during which Quaker ministers traveled to share religious insights. At least once a week, some itinerant Friend would be made welcome in the spare room.

Such visitors presented a more exciting religion than Rufus might have otherwise received. When his father spoke at meeting, Edwin Jones always said pretty much the same thing, something about "making a little heaven on the way to Heaven." Many visitors, however, told valiant stories from Quaker history—about William Penn being thrown in Newgate Prison for preaching on a London street or Philadelphia abolitionist Lucretia Mott walking arm in arm with a black woman into the face of a proslavery mob. Rufus determined to be that sort of Quaker.

Jones graduated from Haverford College in 1885, finishing his undergraduate work in three years and using his senior year to begin a master's degree. After graduation, he taught at a Quaker boarding school until 1893, when he received two offers that arrived almost simultaneously. One was to teach at Haverford, the other to edit *Friends Review*, a weekly Quaker magazine. He took both jobs.

Jones taught at Haverford—psychology, philosophy, ethics, biblical literature and Christian thought—for more than forty years, retiring in 1934. He continued to live at 2 College Circle until his death.

As a teacher, Jones was not a rote deliverer of facts. Colleges that overemphasized information, he believed, forgot their primary purpose "to make moral and spiritual persons." Initially excited by the new field of psychology and its focus on the "inner man," he was disappointed when the profession began to emphasize "body facts." In his class, one lecture on "the physiological basis of psychology" sufficed.

Students loved him. "The philosophers…are too much like the economists," wrote one student to his father, "except a rare few like 'Woofus' who realize that 'character is higher than intellect.'"

Publicly, Jones was best known as a writer and philosopher. *Friends Review* (later the *American Friend*), shaky when he took over, became a tool to spread his idea that religion should be a force for good. It was Jones's way of implementing his boyhood ambition.

Jones worked to mend the Quakers' nineteenth-century schisms. Rather than take sides, he made the *Friend* a forum for all, which had the happy result of broadening its popularity. "His confidence in God's will that all his children be one," wrote biographer Elizabeth Cazden, "is revealed in the way Rufus Jones went about dealing with this situation."

Believing that "truth is not often advanced by religious controversy," Jones never attacked anyone. The *Friend* stayed neutral, for instance, about whether Quakers should have paid pastors. Instead, he simply spoke strongly what he himself believed. And because he felt that disagreements were best resolved by people getting to know one another, he traveled more than ten thousand miles annually.

Jones considered Quaker condescension toward the military counterproductive. In 1942, in Wallingford, he met a naval officer recuperating from wounds received when his ship was sunk at the Battle of Midway. The officer was horrified by war but felt that Japanese atrocities required it. Jones listened to his story and replied, "There are conscientious objectors, but there are also conscientious participants."

The officer, Arnold E. True, became an admiral. He also joined a Quaker meeting in California and, in 1970, came out of retirement to condemn the "immoral" Vietnam War and testified before Congress against the CIA's covert assassination program, Operation Phoenix.

In 1917, Jones was the immediate choice to lead the newly formed AFSC's effort to place conscientious objectors in community service. During World War I, about six hundred Quakers worked in France, mostly in hospitals. After the war, AFSC feeding programs in Germany saved 1.2 million children from starvation. In many German cities, streets where feeding centers were located are still called "Quakerstrasse."

At least some of those children, it seems safe to say, grew up to be Nazis.

In November 1938, when AFSC learned of *Kristallnacht*, officials' first worry was that the Jews—now forbidden to shop in Gentile stores—would starve. Jones and a colleague visited the U.S. State Department, which encouraged a fact-finding trip. Germany's ambassador told the Friends that their top priority should be Jewish immigration.

On December 2, Jones and two colleagues sailed from New York aboard the *Queen Mary*. They'd tried to leave without publicity that might force the Nazis to dismiss these outsiders. But in the middle of the ocean, Jones got a ship-to-shore phone call from the *Philadelphia Record*, whose reporter pieced together the story. "Friends Society Sends Mission to Intercede for German Jews," read the headline.

Joseph Goebbels ridiculed their coming: "We hope [the Quakers] will make themselves known when they are here," read an editorial in his newspaper. "Then we will know, you see, when to begin to quake—quake duly before the Quakers from the U.S.A. Don't expect us to take them seriously." (The *Chicago Daily News* retorted, "That is a good joke, is it not, about the warlike and iron-willed Nazis knowing when to quake before the gentle Quaker pacifists who fed them in their hour of need? Yes, a very good joke. Ha, ha, ha! Ha, ha, ha, ha—ha—ha—")

Hitler wouldn't see them. Goebbels wouldn't see them. The U.S. embassy said that the Gestapo might listen if they could offer a solution. And the only solution of interest, they heard again, would be one that removed Jews. Hjalmar Schacht, a German treasury official, proposed that the Quakers support his plan to pay for Jewish immigration with a fund created by confiscating Jewish property.

If fifty thousand Jews a year could be accepted by other countries, said Schacht, it would solve the problem. "Be quick," he urged, "for nobody knows what happens in this country tomorrow."

It seemed the thing to do. So, one month after *Kristallnacht*, Jones and his friends found themselves deep within the massive eighteenth-century former palace that was Gestapo headquarters, looking across a table at two Heydrich underlings. They assured the Germans that Quakers represented no government or party, reminded them of the feeding program twenty years earlier and asked permission to provide relief and organize immigration. The underlings withdrew to confer with Heydrich.

"During this awesome period," Jones later wrote, "we bowed our heads and entered upon a time of deep meditation and prayer—the only Quaker meeting ever held in the Gestapo."

At length, Heydrich's men returned. "Everything you have asked as been granted," said Obersturmbannführer Kurt Lischka (1909–1987), who would be convicted in 1979 for his role in Jewish deportations but was then simply helping the elderly Jones with his coat. Jones thought the Nazis less icy than when the meeting commenced, writing that they "shook our hands with goodbye wishes and with a touch of gentleness."

The plan didn't last long. Schacht was fired one month later, and his immigration plan died. But Quakers continued to move about Germany to assist those willing and able to leave.

A story seldom told, according to historian William Rubinstein, is that 72 percent of German Jews—and 83 percent of their children—escaped the Holocaust. Most left in the year following *Kristallnacht*. More might have lived had more countries been willing to accept them. The United States refused to increase its twenty-six thousand annual quota for German immigration and interpreted its existing laws so narrowly that only half of the quota was used. England, in contrast, bent its immigration laws to admit more than ten thousand Jewish children as "tourists."

Among them was Ruth Vogel Schwartz of Dresden, whose father put her on a Quaker transport to England in 1939. "We joined dozens of children on the rail station platform," recalled Schwartz.

"Representatives of the Quakers arranged the loading of luggage, took constant roll calls and moved groups of children in front of the specific railroad cars they would occupy." Their families claimed the children after the war.

Not a bad return just for talking with creeps.

Extreme NIMBY

Lower Merion didn't invent NIMBYism. There are way too many competitors in the not-in-my-backyard game to win that title. But a 2006 school district proposal (eventually scrapped) to buy a lot in Philadelphia to park its school buses—thus sparing residents from having to see, smell or hear them—did express a certain sort of continuity.

Since at least the mid-nineteenth century, the essence of Main Line life has been all about its distance from the smelly, noisy facts of life.

Percival Roberts (1857–1943) would have understood perfectly. In 1939, to express his dismay with big government treating him as a mere mortal, Roberts demolished the Gladwyn mansion that he'd spent $3 million (1902) to build.

The problem? Actually, Roberts had two. First, the Lower Merion health inspector had insisted that milk from Roberts's herd of Ayrshire cattle be pasteurized as the law required before it was sold. Second, the township had built an incinerator along the Schuylkill River to dispose of residents' trash. And Roberts could see the smokestack from his estate. Ick!

Roberts was known locally as the "baron" of Pencoyd, the farm passed down from his Welsh ancestor, John Roberts (1648–1724). Originally, the estate had run west from the Schuylkill River along City Avenue and north to Conshohocken State Road. Originally 160 acres, it was expanded over the years. By the time he left Lower Merion in a huff, Roberts's landholdings totaled 539 acres.

In 1852, Roberts's father, Percival Sr. (1830–1898), and his cousin, Algernon, started the Pencoyd Iron Works at the edge of the family property.

Built by iron magnate Percival Roberts, Penshurst cost $3 million in 1902 and was sold to a demolition company for $1,000 in 1939. Lower Merion annoyed Roberts by building an incinerator nearby and citing his dairy for health violations. *Lower Merion Historical Society.*

The factory, located on the Schuylkill, initially manufactured axles for railroad cars. In 1859, however, Pencoyd began to manufacture and erect iron bridges. At this, the company became famous.

Pencoyd bridges were erected over the Delaware at Easton and Philadelphia, and one still spans the Potomac River at Harpers Ferry, West Virginia. Among its greatest coups, however, was a U.S. government contract to erect bridges along Beale's Wagon Road. The road was named for Lieutenant Edward Beale who, in 1857, charted a route—later designated Route 66—linking Fort Smith, Arkansas, to Fort Defiance, Arizona.

That was a lot of bridges. So, Percival Jr. grew up quite comfortably in the Roberts's much expanded 1683 mansion, which stood on the City Line Avenue site later occupied by Saks Fifth Avenue. After graduating from Episcopal Academy and, in 1876, from Haverford College, Roberts joined Pencoyd Iron as a clerk. While learning the business from the bottom up, he also did graduate work in metallurgy and chemistry at Penn.

Roberts learned the business very well. On paper, he was only the owner's son. But in fact, when Percival Sr. died in 1898, Roberts had already been the company's chief manager and strategist for many years.

It was Roberts, for instance, who—with a simple exchange of cable telegrams—sold to British general Lord Henry Kitchener an iron bridge that allowed Great Britain to reconquer the Sudan. In 1884, Muslim rebels led by Muhammad Ahmad al-Mahdi—the Mahdi, for short—had overwhelmed and slaughtered General Charles Gordon and his army at Khartoum. The English wanted revenge.

Though intensely proud of his Ayrshire cattle, Percival Roberts shut down his dairying operation rather than comply with a health inspector's demand that he pasteurize his milk. *Lower Merion Historical Society.*

In 1898, Kitchener's army was marching north along the west bank of the Nile toward the market town of Omdurman, headquarters of the Mahdist movement. To get there, Kitchener needed to cross the Atbara River, a tributary of the Nile. British firms insisted that the bridge could not be built in anything less than two years. Roberts wired Kitchener that his company could do it in forty-two days and sent over a ship loaded with steel girders and six Pencoyd engineers to put them together.

Kitchener crossed the Atbara on schedule and reached Omdurman in September. There, in Great Britain's last great cavalry assault, the English killed three thousand Sudanese and wounded another four thousand. Young Winston Churchill, covering the battle for an English newspaper, wept and wrote to his mother: "Our victory was disgraced by the inhuman slaughter of the wounded and Lord Kitchener was responsible for this."

Kitchener razed the tomb of the Mahdi, who had died fifteen years earlier. Then—depending on which version one hears—he either burned the corpse and threw the ashes in the Nile or turned the Mahdi's skull into a drinking cup with which to toast Gordon's memory. The tomb was rebuilt in the mid-twentieth century as a shrine, and Sudanese memories of British occupation remain less than positive.

In thanks, Kitchener sent to each Pencoyd engineer an iron plaque reading: "I congratulate the American foremen and workmen on the excellent success which has crowned their efforts in the erection of this bridge in the heart of Africa." One of these plaques is now in the collection of the Lower Merion Historical Society.

Described at his death as "the greatest practical steel man in the world," Roberts knew where he wanted to take Pencoyd Iron. After burying his

Penshurst Farms dairy was advanced for its day. Owner Roberts never reused milk bottles, experimented with disposable cartons and sequestered his cattle. But he refused to pasteurize his milk, something he thought unnecessary for quality products. *Lower Merion Historical Society.*

father, Roberts merged the company with a competitor, the American Bridge Company, which in turn merged with U.S. Steel in 1902. Roberts then joined the board of U.S. Steel, where he served with some of his era's leading robber barons: J.P. Morgan, John D. Rockefeller, Charles Schwab and Henry Clay Frick.

From Philadelphia to Malvern

In 1885, Roberts married Bessye W. Frothingham of Boston and built a Victorian frame house on a hill overlooking the ironworks. Upon becoming sole proprietor of Pencoyd Iron, however, the Victorian must have seemed too modest. So, in 1901, Roberts announced that he would build a new $50,000 home with a $50,000 conservatory. Bessye liked to garden.

As it turned out, the house and grounds cost Roberts much, much more. Bessye fell in love with Edward VII's English estate, Sandringham House. So, the couple set out to duplicate it with the help of a Boston architectural firm and a local contractor, George F. Payne & Co., which Roberts subsequently accused of substandard work and fired. (The company took Roberts to court and won a $100,000 settlement.) When finished, Penshurst boasted seventy-five rooms with teak floors, antique English paneling and a marble-floored reception hall dominated by vast stained-glass windows. An electric generating plant on Mill Creek powered the house.

For Bessye, Roberts scattered Greek statuary throughout the property and dug a small lake that perfectly reflected the house. Specially chosen trees were arranged in the landscape to resemble impressionist paintings. For himself, Roberts built several dairy barns for his beloved Ayrshire cattle. Like many successful businessmen of his era, Roberts liked to think of himself as a farmer, albeit one who employed dozens of farmworkers and on-staff veterinarians.

Roberts was extremely fussy in his dairy operation. Though required to quarantine his imported cattle only a few months, he sequestered them a year and required that visitors wear sterile smocks and masks to view them. Roberts never reused milk bottles and experimented with disposable cardboard containers. For him, it was a matter of pride that many Main Liners preferred his unpasteurized milk.

"Roberts believed that only inferior milk required pasteurization," said Jerry Francis, president of the Lower Merion Historical Society.

Percival and Bessye Roberts weren't the only people to live this way. The Main Line was populated by business leaders whose factories provided jobs and pollution for Philadelphia. Baldwin Locomotive, for instance, was located in Spring Garden, but its president, Samuel Vauclain, lived in Radnor. The Pennsylvania Railroad's Broad Street Station faced city hall, but its president, Alexander Cassatt, lived in Haverford. Sun Oil built its tank farms along the lower Schuylkill and a refinery in Marcus Hook, but its owner, Joseph Norton Pew, built his mansion, Glenmede, on a hill in Bryn Mawr.

Credit the region's prevailing wind, said Francis. Then, as now, it sweeps down from the northwest and pushes Philadelphia's exhaust into New Jersey. The result? Wealthy Main Liners didn't have to smell what their factories' smokestacks were puffing out.

"They knew it wasn't healthy down there [in Philadelphia]," said Francis. "That's why the Main Line has always made such a selling point of its quality of life."

Roberts ignored the first notices from George Webster Grim, Lower Merion's health inspector, that selling unpasteurized milk was against the law. Roberts sat on the board of U.S. Steel and other leading corporations! More than the president—and certainly more than Congress—he and those of his class directed the U.S. economy and, thus, the lives of millions of Americans. His Atbara bridge had saved Britain's empire. He didn't have to listen to some township pipsqueak health inspector.

But then the fines started, and eventually Roberts gave up his dairy business. He reduced the Ayrshire herd to a few select specimens.

The final straw came in the late 1930s when Lower Merion announced that an incinerator would replace an open dump on North Woodbine Avenue.

Officials insisted that the facility would produce no smoke and no odor, but Roberts fought it to the state supreme court, where he lost in March 1939. Julius Zieget, president of the Lower Merion commission, hailed the township's victory: "No matter whether people are rich or poor, big or little, they are going to get equal treatment by this township." But that was the era of the New Deal, when government was coming to be seen as the friend of the little guy.

Probably Roberts knew that he would lose. He'd auctioned the contents of Penshurst the previous month. That summer, he sold the house to a demolition company for $1,000. Demolition began in the fall. The site was later redeveloped and, in 2010, Penshurst's only remains were its gates on Conshohocken State Road.

Percival and Bessye moved into a suite at the Bellevue Stratford Hotel for a few months; then, with their point made, they left town to spend their final years in warmer climates.

Leaving is always a NIMBY's last option.

1939
THE SOUND OF DRINKER

Americans of the early twenty-first century are less likely to be joiners than Americans of fifty years earlier. Rather than join bowling leagues, for instance, we are "bowling alone"—volunteering less, voting less and socializing less with our fellow citizens.

As an example of what's lost when interaction declines, consider Henry S. Drinker Jr. (1880–1965) of Merion. By day, Drinker was a heavyweight Philadelphia lawyer who argued cases before the U.S. Supreme Court. But his evenings were devoted to music. Drinker's weekly singing parties regularly attracted crowds to his home for dinner and Bach cantatas. These gatherings also helped give the world the singing Trapp family, whose *Sound of Music* story was told in a 1965 film and is still seen onstage by 600,000 people annually.

When the Trapps arrived at Ellis Island with four dollars in 1939, Drinker helped the family through immigration red tape and lent them a house across Merion Road from his own. Baron Georg Trapp, Maria (his "singing nun" second wife) and their ten children lived in Merion until the mid-1940s.

"The entire success of their eventual singing achievements was based upon the solid foundation of their Philadelphia years," wrote Victoria Donohue, a local historian.

Born in Philadelphia, Drinker was the eldest son of a renaissance man who was successively a mining engineer, lawyer and, beginning in 1905, president of Lehigh University. The Lehigh job required Henry Sr. to move his family to Bethlehem. But when he retired, they promptly returned "home" to Merion.

The *Sound of Music* Trapp family—gathered here in Merion for their traditional Austrian coffee hour—lived with lawyer Henry Drinker in the 1940s after he rescued them from immigration red tape and bankrolled their early tours. *Lower Merion Historical Society.*

The Drinkers were what the nineteenth century called an "interesting" family. Henry Jr.'s sister, Catherine Drinker Bowen, wrote biographies of Oliver Wendell Holmes and John Adams, plus *Miracle at Philadelphia*, the inside story of the Constitutional Convention. His brothers, Cecil and Philip, were professors at Harvard Medical School. A maternal aunt, Cecilia Beaux, painted Edith (Mrs. Teddy) Roosevelt's White House portrait and, as an artist, was considered the equal of John Singer Sargent. A daughter, Ernesta Drinker Ballard (1920–2005), was a founding member of the National Organization for Women (NOW) and a horticulturist who helped make the Philadelphia Flower Show an international event.

All Drinker children took music lessons. But only Henry, who played piano, and Catherine, violin, became passionate about it. A family story has Henry practicing in summer beside an open window as his friends hit baseballs outside until—in "misery," wrote Bowen—he put his hands over his face and cried, "Oh, Ma! I wish I didn't love music so much!" Beaux painted nine-year-old Henry at the piano, legs dangling. Music even led the siblings to attend church twice on Sundays. In Bethlehem, after sitting through a Presbyterian service—with its "awful, sentimental" music—the two rushed up the hill to hear the choir sing the Episcopal offertory.

"This was expensive; it meant two collections in one day," wrote Bowen, who recalled the bishop teasing them for deserting the Presbyterians. "Harry [told] him the Presbyterians didn't know the word B-a-c-h and sang hymns with bad melodic lines that jumped and kicked."

Still, Drinker doesn't seem to have entertained any silly ideas about a music career. He graduated from Haverford College and studied law at Harvard and Penn before joining the Philadelphia firm of Dickson, McCouch & Glasgow in 1904. Founded in 1849, the firm still exists as Drinker, Biddle & Reath—renamed, in part, for the man who would be a dominant force there for fifty years.

Drinker built his reputation representing management in labor disputes, which he usually won. However, he lost his most famous case, *United Mine Workers* v. *Coronado Coal Co.*, in which he had argued that a labor union should be treated as an illegal trust. Drinker also vehemently disapproved of the New Deal and "the blight of the Sherman [Anti-Trust] Act and the unnecessary and irrational attacks on great enterprise in the United States." Bowen recalled that he was "ashen" on Election Day 1936, when Franklin Roosevelt was reelected.

In the McCarthy era, though, Drinker threw his firm into the defense of men and women suspected of Communist leanings. Drinker lawyers working pro bono won several victories, including *United States v. Deutch*, in which the Supreme Court reversed the conviction of a Penn graduate student who refused to name his political associates. According to Bowen, when a client insisted that the firm stop defending "Commies," Drinker told the man he "could take his business where he liked."

But even as Drinker worked eighty-hour weeks, he found another twenty hours for music. He had built his Merion house around a music room large enough for two grand pianos, a Hammond organ and 150 people. He rose daily at 7:00 a.m. to give his children music lessons before taking the train into town; in the evening, he began pounding the piano almost as soon as he walked in the door. But the truth was that—passion aside—Drinker lacked the raw talent to play Brahms or Schumann piano quintets as he knew they should be played. He was frustrated.

A guest suggested choral singing as an alternative. As an experiment, Drinker invited 20 or so musical friends to dinner without their instruments. They sang Brahms's *Liebeslieder-Walzer*. "The evening generated much excitement," wrote Bowen. "Harry was in heaven." These gatherings eventually grew to 150 people, who gathered each Sunday and sang from 5:30 to 9:30 p.m., with an hour off in the middle for dinner. The group continued for thirty years.

One evening, a skeptical Willem van der Walle—a harpist under Toscanini—joined the group to sing Bach's Choral Fantasia from Cantata 93 and professed himself astonished. "The sound," he told Drinker, "is *good*."

A need for material led Drinker to the realization that many classics had never been properly translated. In Bach's cantatas, for instance, available translations clumsily replaced multi-syllable German words with single-syllable English equivalents, causing singers to lose the flow. So, with a German scholar at his elbow, Drinker rearranged the text so that every English syllable was printed with the corresponding note. For this work, Drinker later received an honorary doctorate from Penn.

Drinker met the Trapps when the Austrian refugees came through Philadelphia on their first U.S. tour. The family had fled Austria in the fall of 1938 after Germany annexed the country. Despite what is shown in the movie, they didn't hike out over the mountains. Instead, the Trapps left by train on what was to be a permanent tour based in Norway. Drinker heard of their talent and invited them to dine and to sing.

The Trapps had only a three-month visa but were impressed by the vast U.S. market. Back in Scandinavia, they applied for a visa extension. Thinking it granted, they returned in October 1939. But they were stopped at Ellis Island by officials who charged, Baron Trapp wrote to Drinker, "that we are not temporary visitors but that we want to veil our real intention to hide somewhere in the country, never to go back." Could Drinker help?

Drinker got the Trapps a six-month visa extension. When it expired, the Germans were in Norway, making return impossible. Drinker also lent them his late parents' house (252 Merion Road) in which to get established. Later, when their bus broke down on a West Coast tour, he used a connection at the Budd Co., a client, to procure a replacement.

"Instead of paying me in cash, pay me in music," Drinker told the Trapps. "And so it happened," Maria Trapp continued. "A most perfect exchange of goods. Each one gave what he had; and we sang for him and with him the master works of the 16th and 17th centuries which he hadn't discovered yet, and both parties were truly happy."

Merion is where the Trapps Americanized. They embraced Thanksgiving but disliked the U.S. Christmas. "It took several Christmas seasons before we understood the connection between Christmas shopping and 'Silent Night'…blaring from loudspeakers," Maria later wrote. At school, the Trapp kids were teased for their lederhosen (breeches) and dirndls (dresses), but for a while, those were the only clothes they owned. Worse than teasing, though, may have been wearing the woolen clothing through Philadelphia summers.

The Main Line was not conducive to the long hikes the Trapps loved. "Every other car stopped and asked whether we didn't want a lift," wrote Maria. "When we…wanted to sit down somewhere for a picnic, a sign on a tree invariably said: 'Private—Keep Out—No Trespassing.'"

The hardest lesson may have come when the Trapps were dropped by their manager. They weren't booking enough concerts. Their music, the Trapps were told, was too long, and American audiences preferred songs in English. And Maria and the girls—with their long skirts, braids and serious expressions—lacked sex appeal. "Can't you get decent store clothes," asked one agent, "so one can see your legs in nylon stockings, get pretty, high-heeled shoes and put a little red on your face and on your lips?" He agreed to represent them if the Trapps paid $5,000 for publicity and advertising.

"I'll lend you half the money if you find somebody for the other half," said Drinker, who promptly phoned a musical friend. In minutes, it was done.

The Trapps tweaked their act a bit and changed its name. The Trapp Family Choir ("too church-y," said the agent) became the Trapp Family Singers. Maria wrote a book, *The Sound of Music*, for publicity. By 1942, they were doing well enough to get a mortgage on a farm in rural, Austria-like Stowe, Vermont, and return Drinker's house keys.

You know the rest. Now, go join something, would you?

1940

AN ACCEPTABLE CORPSE

All corpses are not created equal. The sight of dead Americans affects us differently than the sight of dead foreigners. The bodies of U.S. soldiers are handled with reverence, while photos of the pulped corpses of our enemies are posted online for gawkers.

It was the same in 1940 when New York artist Alfred D. Crimi (1900–1994) submitted his proposal for a mural at the new Wayne post office in Radnor. The design, intended to depict the highlights of General Anthony Wayne's career, included a dead British soldier. That was logical, since Wayne was responsible for the deaths of many British soldiers during the Revolutionary War.

But with the Battle of Britain raging and U.S. sympathies overwhelmingly pro-English, that wouldn't do. After "input" from federal bureaucrats, Crimi replaced the dead Englishman with a dead Indian, which bothered no one.

"Today, you can't even name a baseball team the Braves without a controversy," said Salvatore Indiviglia, Crimi's former assistant, who in 2005 was retired and living on Long Island. "But, then, nobody thought about it."

Radnor learned in the late 1930s that it would be getting a new post office to replace the temporary space it had used for more than ten years. From 1885 until the building was demolished in 1927, the post office had rented space at Lancaster and South Wayne Avenues. Wayne Art Center officials lobbied successfully for a colonial-style (not—horrors!—contemporary) building, and the current red brick post office was dedicated in 1941. If anyone locally had concerns about the mural, however, no record of it seems to have been kept.

A dead British redcoat was supposed to lie at Anthony Wayne's feet in this representation of his career at the Wayne Post Office. But in 1940, the Battle of Britain was raging, and we were on England's side, so that wouldn't do. *Mark E. Dixon.*

Art in federal buildings was then in the hands of the Fine Arts section of the Federal Works Agency, a Depression-era department that also administered the Work Projects Administration (WPA). The WPA was conceived in 1935 to employ people on relief—including artists—on useful projects.

In 1940, the Fine Arts section announced a nationwide competition to choose an artist to design and paint a fresco in the new Social Security building (now home of the Department of Health and Human Services) in Washington, D.C. The winner was Lithuanian-born Ben Shahn (1898–1969), whose fresco, *The Meaning of Social Security*, continued the artist's favored theme of social injustice. "I feel," Shahn wrote the agency, "that the whole Social Security idea is one of the real fruits of democracy."

A secondary goal of the competition, however, was to identify artists for other projects. Among them was Crimi.

"The thing is, when Shahn got the Social Security job, he had never painted a fresco," said Indiviglia, who explained that the judges' decision had been based on twenty-four- by twenty-four-inch pencil sketches of the artists' proposed designs. "Shahn didn't know what to do, so he ended up coming to Crimi, one of the foremost fresco painters in the United States, to learn how to paint fresco."

Born in the village of San Fratello in Sicily, Crimi was the son of a stonemason whose family immigrated to New York when he was nine. An older brother had been killed while quarrying stone. Their brokenhearted mother, Maria, wanting a change of scenery, lobbied Crimi's father, Filadelfio, to join relatives in America. In Manhattan, Alfred started out doing posters for school elections and then moved on to sign painting, commercial and furniture decorations and church murals.

Crimi owed his success to two decisions. First was his decision to return to Italy for a year to learn fresco. Murals were popular in the 1920s, but most Americans didn't understand the difference between simple wall painting and fresco, which is more durable because the paint is applied in wet plaster. Crimi, though, knew that fresco's maintenance-free virtues would be attractive to building owners and help win contracts. He took accelerated courses at Rome's Scuola Preparatoria Alle Arti Ornamentali and spent the rest of his year abroad sightseeing.

Any nostalgia Crimi might have felt for his old home was dashed when he visited his brother's grave and found that it had been sold to a wealthy local family and reused. "I was informed that the graves of the poor are opened after 10 years, the remains exhumed and placed in a common ossuary," Crimi wrote in his 1987 autobiography. Thereafter, he considered himself fully an American.

Crimi's second fateful decision, in 1933, was to apply to the WPA. Though he had struggled through the early years of the Depression, Crimi nevertheless felt that a simple dole was "degrading." The new federal program, however, required that he produce as well as receive and was therefore honorable. The decision made his career. In December 1933, he reported to the Whitney Museum in New York, where his two sample canvases were rated a "good performance." The following July, Crimi was hired to paint murals at a new aquarium in Key West, Florida.

"The publicity Key West was receiving from all parts of the country attracted…artists, writers, actors, politicians and other prominent personalities," wrote Crimi. "I met more people of renown than I ever had in my entire life." He chatted up anarchist Carlo Tesca, drank with Hemingway and ate with writer John Dos Passos. Most important, perhaps, he spent hours with Edward Bruce, director of the federal public works project, who was impressed by his knowledge of fresco.

From Philadelphia to Malvern

Back in New York, Crimi was hired to paint five frescos on the history of medicine at Harlem Hospital. (Ignorant of the subject, he watched several operations, including a seven-hour brain surgery) Next came the main post office in Washington, D.C., where he was one of six artists selected from more than three hundred in a nationwide competition. Crimi created two panels—*Parcel Post* and *Modern Post Office*. Next came a commission from Manhattan's Rutgers Presbyterian Church to paint a mural of Christ's last appearance to the apostles.

Crimi was a liberal in a 1930s sense of standing up for the little guy. Though he had Old World manners—always removing his hat in a woman's presence, for instance—he instinctively resented injustice. In the fifth grade, he resisted a teacher who was smacking him with a ruler in the mistaken belief that he had thrown a spitball. Crimi broke the ruler and shoved the woman away, inadvertently sending her tumbling over a desk. In Italy, he comforted an old friend whose son was shunned by relatives for leaving Catholicism to join the Seventh Day Adventists. "I believe there is one God for all the world," he told the woman. "Your son kept his faith and it is for others to respect that." In Washington, he refused a union official's attempt to extort an above-scale salary for a plasterer's assistant—even when the man put a fist in his face.

"He was always a gentleman, never anti anything," said Indiviglia, a fellow Italian whose decision to enlist during World War II disturbed Crimi because it meant that he would fight other Italians. "But he always admired people who were sincere in whatever they were doing." Indiviglia was an interrogator in Italy, a combat artist in Vietnam and, later, a commander in the U.S. Naval Reserve.

But Crimi was not one to be pushed around. In 1945, when the Rutgers church painted over his 1938 mural because a new minister objected to Christ's bare chest—and brushed off his protests—Crimi sued. He lost. As a property owner, the church was within its rights, the court ruled. But the case galvanized opinion within the art world and, in 1983, Crimi testified before the New York Assembly, which subsequently passed a "Moral Rights Bill" to protect artists. Today, the widely held consensus is that artists retain rights to their works even when owned by others.

Crimi also knew when to pick his battles. After losing the Social Security job, he gratefully accepted the opportunity to do murals at small post offices in Northampton, Massachusetts, and in Wayne. After a brief trip to Radnor to inspect the location on the east wall of the lobby, Crimi returned to the studio with a set of specs and the news that the theme would be the life of General Anthony Wayne.

"He asked me to do the artistic and library research," said Indiviglia, who dug into books to identify appropriate apparel and the highlights of Wayne's life. The sketch subsequently submitted for *Anthony Wayne, General, Surveyor and Gentleman Farmer* showed Wayne planting a small tree, peering through a surveying level and, in full military uniform, standing over the corpse of a British soldier.

The dead Brit, said Indiviglia, was a reference to the 1779 battle at Stony Point, New York, where Wayne led 1,300 men in a night bayonet attack against a British position, which fell after about thirty minutes. Similar to the 1777 British bayonet assault on Wayne's position at Paoli, the attack earned him a gold medal from Congress and the nickname "Mad Anthony."

At some point during the planning—Indiviglia doesn't recall exactly when—Crimi ordered that the corpse's red uniform be painted green, a color commonly worn by Hessians, the German troops hired by the British to help subdue their rebellious colonies. "It's only a guess, but an educated one, I think, that he got word that the government didn't want a dead redcoat," said Indiviglia. "You don't offend your allies by bringing up the unpleasant past."

A dead Hessian, however, didn't work historically or artistically. There had been no Hessians at Stony Point. Because fewer Americans remember Hessian green than British scarlet, there was also real danger that the painting would confuse viewers. And, sure enough, Crimi got a carefully worded memo from the Federal Works Agency that the green-jacketed corpse was "unexplained." So, Crimi followed the path of least resistance. He gave the body reddish skin and feathers in its hair. This worked historically because Wayne had fought and defeated Indians in present-day Ohio in the 1790s.

Alas, the solution eliminated any specific reference to the Revolution. But that was less important than that the U.S. Post Office's official representation of the career of Anthony Wayne include an appropriate corpse.

1950
DOCTORS, GENERALS AND POLITICIANS

Doctors, politicians and generals all bury their mistakes. Strangely, though, only the reputations of physicians seem to suffer.

Douglas MacArthur (1880–1964) and Harry Truman (1884–1972), for instance, are remembered mostly for winning World War II, not for the Korean War blunders that killed seven alumni of Tredyffrin-Easttown High School. But those seven deaths document what happened.

Admiral Omar Bradley mostly blamed MacArthur, whose insistence that China would not join the conflict turned a six-month scuffle into a three-year war. MacArthur's pride, said Bradley, made him "willing to propel us into all-out war with Red China, and possibly the Soviet Union, igniting World War III and a nuclear holocaust."

But it was Truman who set the stage for war by inviting Stalin to invade Korea in 1945. The events that doomed New Centerville native Ray McLaughlin (1930–1950) began at Potsdam, where Stalin and Truman met for their final wartime conference. Anticipating a U.S. invasion of Japan, Truman pushed the Russian dictator to attack the Japanese wherever he could.

Also, in February 1945, McLaughlin's father, Eli, was granted a divorce on grounds of desertion. Mildred McLaughlin, he testified, had been "running around with another man" since 1936. The same month, Ray's older brother, Herbert, was so seriously wounded at Iwo Jima that he would still be hospitalized in 1950. Ray, one of thirteen children, was fifteen years old and living with his father on Walker Road. After his graduation in 1948, Ray would be the fourth in his family to enlist.

Stalin had previously stayed out of the Pacific war. But he couldn't resist an invitation to take Korea, which Japan had occupied since 1905. Soviet troops invaded the country in August. But then U.S. thinking changed. The atomic bombing of Hiroshima and Nagasaki meant that we no longer required Russian help. Word came down from the War Department to create some sort of division between communist and noncommunist forces.

On August 10, 1945, two U.S. colonels looked at an old school map of Korea, noticed the country narrowed at its midpoint and chose the thirty-eighth parallel. Stalin accepted. The Koreans, who had endured Japanese occupation but never the division of their country, were not consulted.

In the south, the United States handed power to Syngman Rhee (1875–1965), a Korean expatriate who had lived in America for forty years, spoke good English and was fiercely anticommunist. In the north, the Russians installed Kim Il Sung (1912–1994), a schoolteacher's son who had joined the communists as a teenager and had spent most of his life fighting the Japanese. (The current dictator, Kim Jong Il, is his son.)

Both Rhee and Sung were democratically challenged, demonstrating similar tendencies to arrest and execute political opponents. Both also announced intentions to rule the entire country. Sung was better equipped to accomplish this goal: Stalin had left him a well-trained, well-equipped, 135,000-man army. Stalin also left 150 T-34 tanks, one of his most effective weapons against the Germans.

By comparison, Rhee was almost unarmed. The United States had withdrawn most of its troops in 1949. Fearing Rhee's intentions, Washington had also rebuffed his requests for air power and tanks. As a result, the North Korean troops who crossed the thirty-eighth parallel in June 1950 required just three days to reach and capture the South Korean capital at Seoul.

McLaughlin had then been in the army two years, assigned to the First Cavalry Division in occupied Japan. It was cushy duty, according to General William Dean, who described these soldiers as "fat and happy in occupation billets, complete with Japanese girlfriends, plenty of beer and servants to shine their boots."

Only one in six was a combat veteran. The U.S. military, which had inducted nearly 10 million men during World War II, had since shrunk to fewer than 600,000. The 1950 army, wrote historian David Halberstam, included many "lured by recruiting officers promising an ideal way to get out of small-town America."

South Korean troops fled. When MacArthur arrived four days after the war began, he was stunned to see thousands retreating without their weapons and, he noted angrily, "not…a wounded man among them."

Also stunned was Truman, who quickly (and incorrectly) concluded that the attack in Korea had been ordered by Stalin and, therefore, meant coming attacks elsewhere. "We are going to fight," Truman told his daughter, Margaret. "By God, I am not going to let them have it." He quickly approved MacArthur's request for a regimental combat team and two divisions. Later, so did Congress.

The North Koreans rolled over the first ill-equipped U.S. troops rushed in from Japan. Casualties in the first week totaled about three thousand killed, wounded and missing. Soon, though, fresh troops and supplies poured into the south-coast port of Pusan, where MacArthur established a defensive perimeter fifty miles wide by one hundred miles long.

On August 30, about three weeks after ninety-eight thousand North Koreans began their assault on the Pusan perimeter, McLaughlin wrote to his father: "Don't worry about me. I'll be all right." Ten days later, he was dead.

With the north's supply lines stretched, MacArthur proposed an amphibious landing on the west coast of Korea to squeeze the enemy massed around Pusan from two sides. It worked. MacArthur landed thirteen thousand marines at Inchon to little resistance and, within two weeks, had recaptured Seoul. Half of the North Korean army was killed or captured. By October 1, South Korean troops were back at the thirty-eighth parallel, crossing into North Korea.

Old China experts had warned that Beijing would not tolerate the conquest of a communist state. In fact, China protested immediately. But nobody wanted to stop in the middle of a rout, least of all MacArthur, who dismissed the increasingly wary British as appeasers.

Douglas MacArthur had not visited the United States since 1937. But his strategic brilliance in World War II had made him a legend at home, and the success at Inchon seemed to have made him a god. But MacArthur also considered himself above taking orders. His most famous utterance, after evacuating the Philippines in 1942, was, "I shall return." (The famously modest Eisenhower might have said, "We shall return.")

Worse, MacArthur was out of date. He thought the Chinese army was still made up of ignorant, barefoot coolies. Meeting with Truman in October, MacArthur promised to "slaughter" any Chinese who entered Korea. Then he returned to his headquarters, in Tokyo.

At least 130,000 Chinese were already in Korea. But even as it took Chinese prisoners, U.S. command denied that anything had changed. Said one of MacArthur's subordinates: "A lot of Mexicans live in Texas."

The Chinese first hit the Americans November 1 when they were deep inside North Korea, about seventy miles from the Chinese border. Three days later, MacArthur admitted that Chinese intervention was "a distinct possibility" but ordered the advance north to continue.

"It was a fateful moment," wrote Halberstam. "By dint of his arrogance, foolishness and vainglory, MacArthur was about to take a smaller war that was already winding down and expand it to include as an adversary a Communist superpower, thereby adding more than two years to its life."

On November 25, the Chinese struck again, this time against U.S. convoys strung out on narrow mountain roads. The Chinese poured down concentrated fire and then attacked in V formations that unfolded to envelop U.S. positions. In the last days of November, five thousand men of the Second Division were killed and wounded.

Tredyffrin-Easttown (T-E) grad John B. Webb (1931–1950) was shot to death December 4 near the Chosin Reservoir, where fifteen thousand marines were assaulted in nighttime attacks by 120,000 Chinese. Six months after graduating high school, Webb was buried on the battlefield, where he died carrying ammunition to a machine gunner. By mid-December, U.S. and allied troops had retreated south of the thirty-eighth parallel.

On December 7, navy pilot Ralph Rogers (1925–1951) of Paoli was killed in a training flight accident in Florida. He was his parents' only child.

On January 4, 1951, Seoul fell again. The next day, Jacob C. Lehman (1927–1951), a former T-E football player whose mother was the Devon postmaster, died in the crash of his air force bomber.

MacArthur blamed the administration. Its restrictions, he insisted, were all that kept him from crushing the Chinese. As Truman was putting out feelers about a truce, his own general provoked China by publicly ridiculing its "exaggerated" military power and advocated the use of atomic weapons. "There is," he wrote the Republican House minority leader, "no substitute for victory."

In March 1951, Truman fired him.

Replacing MacArthur was Matt Ridgway (1895–1993), called by his subordinates "the man who came to dinner" because he seemed to be everywhere. Ridgway took the high ground along the thirty-eighth parallel and equipped U.S. forces with the tools to hold this line: flares to illuminate the Chinese during night attacks and artillery to mow them down.

Ridgway's own personal bravery rallied the demoralized army: "He'd stand out in the middle of the road and urinate," recalled fellow general James Gavin. "I'd say, 'Matt, get the hell out of there. You'll get shot!' No! He was defiant. Even with his penis, he was defiant."

Negotiations began in July 1951 and dragged on for two years as shooting continued. (Half of all casualties occurred during the talks.) Killed during this period were T-E grads Edward Baumgard (1931–1951) of Frazer in August 1952; Isaiah Keith (1930–1951) of Paoli in November 1952; and Willie M. Francis (1931–1953).

Francis died on July 24, three days before the armistice was signed. On July 22, he wrote to his sister: "We are getting good news about the peace and I hope to be back in the states by the end of the year." The names of Francis and the rest are on a plaque in the lobby of TEHS's successor, Conestoga High School.

MacArthur, Truman, Stalin, Sung and Rhee all died in bed.

1953

BLAMING THE MESSENGER

The media has always been a handy scapegoat.

In Lower Merion, for instance, writer James A. Michener (1907–1997) has been damned since the mid-twentieth century for a magazine article that so besmirched one neighborhood that its name had to be changed.

In fact, though, renaming West Manayunk to Belmont Hills didn't occur until three years after the article appeared, and then for unrelated reasons. In the 1950s, Americans were streaming out of big cities. "Belmont Hills" simply sounded more suburban. Changing, said residents, would make it clear that their community was not part of Philadelphia. It might even raise property values.

West Manayunk "sounds cheesy, like a hick town," one resident told the *Main Line Times* in 1953. "Why should we be affiliated with Manayunk?" Plus, Michener himself never insulted West Manayunk, though he quoted someone who did, sorta.

Manayunk—Lenape for "where we go to drink"—was the name given in 1824 to an area previously known as Falls of Schuylkill and Flat Rock. Incorporated in 1840, Manayunk developed into a well-known manufacturing district after the Schuylkill Navigation Co. built a dam, canal and locks and began selling water power rights to mill owners.

The Lower Merion (west) side of the river had no similar identity. Two main hills were dubbed, respectively, Ashland Hill, after the estate of an early landowner, and Narrows Hill, after the channel that separated the riverbank from Jones Island. The flat riverbank, meanwhile, was called Roslagen, for

According to local lore, writer James Michener insulted the ethnic neighborhood of West Manayunk—seen here from Philadelphia—so badly that it changed its name to Belmont Hills. In reality, 1950s residents just wanted a more suburban image. *Lower Merion Historical Society.*

reasons apparently unrecorded, though the name is also used to describe a coastal area in Sweden.

"West Manayunk" came into use in 1838 when the Reading Railroad built a train station using the name near today's Belmont interchange.

In the nineteenth century, West Manayunk's walkable proximity to the mills turned it into a convenient residential area. Italians and Albanians were dominant, and enough kept goats that, for a while, the area was nicknamed "Goat Hill."

Socially and culturally, West Manayunk looked east to Philadelphia rather than west to the WASPy Main Line. Residents worked in blue-collar jobs and retained many Old World customs.

In 1979, Patricia Puhl wrote in a local newspaper about the neighborhood in which she had grown up a half century before: "The women were dressed totally in black and almost always walked with a man at their sides," she said. "The men were the dominant heads of the families. Many of them walked the hills wearing a turbanlike headgear used for carrying food."

West Manayunkers knew who they were. According to historian Geraldine A. Fisher, the immigrants who worked Philadelphia's nineteenth-century mills came at a time when militant labor ideas were prevalent in Europe. That background, combined with oppressive working conditions, helped create a strong working-class identity. Philadelphia's first labor unions were organized in Manayunk, with the first strikes occurring in the late 1820s. West Manayunk was those workers' backyard.

When Michener came to town, he had recently won a Pulitzer for *Tales of the South Pacific* (1946), his first book, and had just published his second, *The Fires of Spring* (1949), a semiautobiographical novel about an orphan who finds professional and romantic success.

Michener's version of his life story was that he never knew his parents, his birthplace or even his birth date. He was adopted by a Doylestown Quaker, graduated from Swarthmore College and went on to teach at a variety of schools, including Harvard. His writing career began during World War II when, as a naval historian, he began to gather material for a collection of short stories.

Later in his career, Michener could afford to turn down hack writing assignments. But in 1949, he agreed to do a profile of the Main Line for *Holiday* magazine, a new (1946) upbeat travel publication. It paid well. There was no shame in it. John Steinbeck and Irwin Shaw also wrote for *Holiday*.

The article itself was pure puffery. In prose accompanied by photographs of stone mansions, debutantes, horses and Quaker meetings, Michener praised the old families who ran the place so well. The article did acknowledge that the Main Line's heyday had passed. Rather than a pile of stone costing millions, he wrote, "today's Main Line aristocrat prefers a $40,000 house. And rather than 30 servants, he strives to get—and keep—one." Overall, Michener depicted a suburban utopia in which most residents wanted, and got, little change.

He could hardly do anything else. *Holiday*'s owner, Curtis Publishing, was based in Philadelphia. Many of its executives lived on the Main Line. Walter D. Fuller, president of Curtis, lived in Penn Valley. Michener hadn't been hired to muckrake.

Michener did not omit Lower Merion's Schuylkill waterfront, where, he wrote, a "somewhat impoverished citizenry lives clinging to the river's edge" despite frequent floods. And then this:

Farther downriver, the cliffside town of West Manayunk perches Pittsburgh-like in the gloom. "It's a disgrace to call that a part of Lower Merion," the Main Liner is likely to protest. "It really belongs to Philadelphia." The school board, however, is determined to provide the best that democracy can afford, and sends the West Manayunk children to the ultralovely Bala-Cynwyd Junior High. "By the time we get them in Lower Merion High," the officials say, "you can't tell them from the others. Good kids, those Manayunkers."

If they read the article at all, most Main Liners quickly threw it aside. The Ehart brothers, publishers of the *Wayne Suburban*, entirely missed the implied slight to blue-collar West Manayunkers. Their editorial merely complained that Michener portrayed all Main Liners as rich. The *Main Line Times* didn't react at all.

But in West Manayunk, there was outrage. At a standing room–only meeting, neighbors demanded an apology from *Holiday* for "slurring" the community and "stigmatizing" the youngsters." In particular, West Manayunkers focused on the implication that their children were not okay until the junior high had processed them to Lower Merion standards. George W.R. Kirkpatrick, principal, appeared to reassure parents that their children were valued.

"Your children have played in our bands…and on our teams," he told the crowd. "The most cooperative students we get in our orchestra come from West Manayunk."

But it wasn't quite enough; West Manayunkers wanted to know whom Michener had interviewed.

"The hill folk," reported the *Times*, "assert that author James A. Michener did not suck the [statement] out of his thumb." A civic association was formed to demand an answer.

Into this stepped Dr. Albert C. Barnes, art collector, original benefactor of the Barnes Museum and local crank. Barnes had hated Michener since learning that, as a Swarthmore student in the 1920s, the writer had lied his way into his Merion art gallery. Barnes was famously distrustful of—and barred from his art gallery—anyone he thought to be an intellectual. College students had virtually no chance to get in, so Michener impersonated a steelworker.

"I don't have much education," he wrote in a letter posted from Pittsburgh, "but I hear you have such a real nice bunch of pictures." That brought a written invitation and a tour guided personally by Barnes. He was furious when he learned the truth.

Now, Barnes drew a parallel between Michener's earlier deception and what he had written for *Holiday*. Michener, he said, was an admitted "liar" and a "phony." When Michener attempted a soothing response, Barnes responded in language that remains unprintable.

"What the h--- do you use for [a handkerchief]?" asked Michener. "Barbed wire?" Retorted Barnes: "Why should I use barbed wire when [you] serve the purpose so well?"

When Michener lectured at Penn, Barnes climbed onstage to harangue him in person. Michener walked out. When Barnes challenged the writer to a debate, Michener ignored him.

Michener declined to identify the official whom he had quoted. "It would be a serious breach of honor for me to tell you that," he wrote one resident. But West Manayunkers' angry letters, he noted, proved that the class distinctions he had described did, in fact, exist. ("The Main Liners despise us," one had writtten, "but you should hear what we think of the Main Liners!")

The uproar continued for a couple of months. In the *Times*, letter writer E.D. Wirt addressed Michener as "Commander, Flying Saucer Squadron" and advised him to "load your crew on your flying saucer and fly off into the blue." Mrs. K.S.C. wrote advising the swells that life was better without servants "in a cozy little six- or seven-room house with one bath, and not being too lazy to do your own work."

Three and a half years went by. In October 1953, West Manayunk's civic association distributed ballots asking residents to choose the existing name or one of four alternatives: Belmont, Belmont Hills, Welsh Hills or Cadwalader. A *Times* editorial, which didn't even mention Michener, joked that the real problem was phonetic.

"It's that 'yunk,'" said the paper. "A check of the words ending in 'unk' discloses that (with the possible exception of 'plunk' and 'spunk') not a one connotes anything good or true or beautiful. Consider, for instance, such approbrious [sic] examples as bunk, drunk, flunk, funk, junk, punk, quidnunc, skunk, slunk and—of course—stunk."

When the 896 votes were counted, 627 voters preferred a new name; of these, 475 chose Belmont Hills. Another 269 favored the old name.

Why? Some West Manayu…er, Belmont Hills residents cited post office confusion. Mail for West Manayunk went to similar addresses across the river.

Mrs. Albert Turtle of Price Street favored Belmont Hills because blueprints for the coming Schuylkill Expressway included a Belmont interchange at the foot of the hill. "Hills" worked, said Rita Terravana of Belmont Avenue, because "we certainly have them around here."

Nobody mentioned Michener.

1955

THE SINGER AND
THE SENATOR

At Radnor High in the 1940s, Anna Moffo (1932–2006) planned to
be a nun. Instead, the cobbler's daughter from Wayne wound up
in Rome as an opera star and actress whose nude scenes in Italian films
titillated '60s filmgoers.

In the end, though, perhaps she served the same cause.

Moffo first sang in Nick Moffo's shoe repair shop located near the Wayne
train station. She sang "Mighty Lak a Rose" in school assemblies but never
had a teacher and never thought of singing as a life. She was an athlete—on
the hockey team and the basketball team and as captain of the tennis team.
According to accounts of her girlhood, her legs got nearly as much attention
at Radnor lacrosse meets as her performances on the field. After graduation
in 1950, there were reportedly nibbles from Hollywood, but Moffo was still
focused on the convent.

Those plans changed when Moffo accepted a scholarship to study
voice and piano at the Curtis Institute of Music. Twenty years later, the
Philadelphia Inquirer described Moffo as the "despair and delight" of less
talented classmates: "Perfect ear. Sang *solfeggio* exercises at sight, even when
her teachers began to transpose them."

With Curtis connections, Moffo sang an aria from *Madame Butterfly* for
Eugene Ormandy (1899–1985), musical director of the Philadelphia
Orchestra. Ormandy made her a soloist, and the reviews were enthusiastic.
"Moffo Boffo," wrote *Inquirer* music critic Samuel L. Singer.

Then J. William Fulbright (1905–1995) entered into her life.

From Philadelphia to Malvern

Anna Moffo of Wayne originally wanted to be a nun, but a great voice took her to the Curtis Institute, and a Fulbright Scholarship took her to Rome, where she sang opera and starred in racy movies. *Radnor Historical Society.*

Fulbright was a U.S. senator from Arkansas. First elected to the House of Representatives in 1942, he'd been an antitrust lawyer at the U.S. Justice Department, a professor at George Washington University Law School and president of the University of Arkansas. Elected to the Senate in 1944, he served until 1974, when he was defeated in the Democratic primary.

In retrospect, Fulbright's Senate career seems schizophrenic. He was a consistent opponent of civil rights legislation in the 1960s and '70s. In foreign relations, however, he was a consistent dove. Fulbright was among the first to criticize the investigations of Senator Joseph McCarthy (R-Wisconsin) into alleged Communist influence and was instrumental in his censure by the Senate. Fulbright opposed creation of the House Un-American Activities Committee. As chair of the Foreign Relations Committee (1959–1974), Fulbright held frequent open hearings to educate the public and to reassert the Senate's influence in long-range policy formulation. An outspoken critic of U.S. military intervention abroad, Fulbright opposed the 1961 Bay of Pigs invasion and the

Anna Moffo's look worked with '60s styles. Her Liz Taylor eyes and dark hair looked great on black-and-white television, and the legs once appreciated by Radnor lacrosse fans were "made for miniskirts." *Radnor Historical Society.*

landing of marines in the Dominican Republic in 1965. He voted for the 1964 Tonkin Gulf Resolution that launched the Vietnam War but later called it the "worst mistake" of his public life and opposed the war's escalation.

Fulbright's leanings were apparent early in his Senate career. In 1946, dismayed by the World War II carnage that had wrecked Europe, the Soviet Union and much of Asia, the freshman senator proposed a scholarship program to increase international understanding. His idea was to bring students from as many countries as possible to study in the United States while sending young Americans to live in and come to know and understand Africa, Asia, Europe, the Western Hemisphere and the Pacific.

Initially, the program was financed by the sale of U.S. war surplus property, supplemented later with United States–held foreign currencies from the sale of grain abroad. In the twenty-first century, the program was supported by an annual Congressional appropriation and run through the U.S. Department of State. There were more than fifty foreign Fulbright commissions, each working with its U.S. counterpart. In 2004, President Bush welcomed to the White House twenty-five Iraqis—nineteen men and six women—who were the first to come to the United States as Fulbright scholars in fourteen years. Starting in 1990, Saddam Hussein had refused to allow Iraqi citizens to leave the country under the Fulbright program.

Starting as a modest effort that, in 1948, brought 35 students and one professor to the United States and sent 65 Americans abroad, the Fulbright program has since sponsored nearly 250,000 students from this and 140 other countries. Oxford professor Robert McCallum called it "the largest and most significant movement of scholars across the earth since the fall of Constantinople in 1453."

Well-known Fulbrighters include U.N. secretary general Boutros Boutros Ghali, Senator Daniel Patrick Moynihan, economist Milton Friedman, writers John Updike and Eudora Welty, actors Stacy Keach and John Lithgow and musician Aaron Copland.

Anna Moffo, however, was the program's first real star. In 1955, she won the Young Artists Auditions and a Fulbright to study at the Accademia di Santa Cecilia in Rome. Her grant didn't cover everything, so she was obliged to find side jobs as an X-ray technician and secretary.

But she also went to auditions. Soon after arriving in Italy, Moffo won the role of Norina in a Spoleto presentation of Donizetti's *Don Pasquale*. The following year, she appeared in an Italian TV production of *Madame Butterfly*, produced by Mario Lanfranchi, whom she married in 1957.

Her career exploded. In 1957, Moffo made her La Scala debut in *Falstaff* and her United States debut as Mimi in Puccini's *La Bohème* at the Lyric Opera of Chicago. In 1959, she debuted at the Metropolitan Opera as Violetta in Verdi's *La Traviata*, returning in the 1960–61 season to sing three new roles: Gilda in Verdi's *Rigoletto*, Adina in Donizetti's *L'Elisir d'Amore* and Liù in *Turandot* with Birgit Nilsson and Franco Corelli.

Moffo even launched other careers. In 1963, after she performed several compositions by young songwriter Richard A. Hundley, Max de Schauensee, the music critic of the *Philadelphia Evening Bulletin*, wrote that the songs showed "a gift for melody and writing for voice." Hundley's career took off.

Moffo had a voice that has been described as "pure and strong" and "creamily seductive." According to opera historian Derek McGovern, "Moffo in her prime had everything that one could wish for in a lyric soprano—warmth, power, thrilling high notes and a beguiling sense of phrasing." Gay writer, self-described "opera queen" and City University of New York English professor Wayne Koestenbaum wrote in 1993 that his love of opera began when he discovered Moffo.

"I had…a timbre against which others would seem too full, too old, too ripe, too controlled," he wrote. "I had chosen a voice that sounded to me like promise and bounty, and compared to this voice, all other aspects of the universe were scrap metal." Koestenbaum's attention later moved to other sopranos, but he remembered his first love in a 1990 poem, "Ode to Anna Moffo":

I think that Anna
Moffo sings,
to this day, in a second,
parallel Met, a hologram of the original
projected in air,
where failing voices continue
to thrive amidst a system of strange geysers
and girders, cables
linking the golden prompter's box
to a sky that burns directly on the stage.

Already famous on stage, Moffo was chosen in 1960 to host a variety show on Italian TV. Every Saturday night, she would sing opera, operetta, Broadway musicals, dance with her own ballet, conduct some of the orchestral selections and even compose some of the music. The *Anna Moffo Show* ran until 1973, and based in part on the exposure she received from it, she was voted one of the ten most beautiful women in Italy.

Anna Moffo's look worked with the fashion styles of the 1960s. Her Liz Taylor eyes and dark hair looked great on black-and-white television. She looked fabulous in sweaters. The lacrosse legs, according to one Philadelphia writer, were "made for miniskirts." Some thought she got by on her looks. But her combination of looks and voice made Moffo one of the first opera divas whose marketing used the eroticism now routinely employed by such stars as violinist Anne Sophie Mutter and jazz singer Diana Krall.

Jet-setters tend to blur together, however. Once, paparazzi at a Rome airport mistook Moffo for Gina Lollobrigida, the similarly bosomed Italian film star. She tried to convince them otherwise, even singing part of an aria.

"Gina!" they cried. "You can sing!"

Moffo also starred in films, including Lanfranchi's *Una storia d'amore* (*A Story of Love*) in which she appeared nude as the married conquest of a casual swinger. "Moffo in the Boffo," said the *New York Daily News*. Clearly, Moffo had gone a long way from Our Lady of Assumption, Radnor's Italian-American Catholic parish. In high school, Moffo's strict parents had not allowed her to date, and she was initially uncomfortable doing romantic scenes onstage. Her slide began at Curtis, when she appeared in *Porgy and Bess* in a red off-the-shoulder dress of which her mother would have not approved. The nudity in her movies, she told an interviewer in 1970, was "not for itself. [It's] nice, when it's part of the story."

Moffo and Lanfranchi divorced in 1972. In 1974, Moffo married Robert Sarnoff, son of broadcast pioneer David Sarnoff. Sarnoff died of cancer in 1997. In 1999, the fortieth anniversary of her debut at the Met, Curtis awarded Moffo an honorary doctorate. She spent her last years in New York.

Among Moffo's biggest fans was J. William Fulbright. In the early days of the Fulbright program, the Arkansas senator was constantly fighting off budget cuts. Moffo served as Fulbright's "shining example. Every time they want to cut back on the Fulbright scholarships, I always say, 'Don't forget, they gave us Anna Moffo.'" Moffo, for her part, responded to every compliment and success, "Most of all, I thank God for my Fulbright!"

She never became a nun, but Moffo accomplished everything for world peace that Fulbright could have hoped. Half a century after first dazzling Rome with her voice and her cleavage, we haven't been to war with Italy since.

1969
GIVING GOOD MEETING

Never underestimate the potential of a good meeting. Tough advice when you're scheduled for back-to-back speakers and a chicken dinner. But there's always the possibility of a *Eureka!* moment like the one that came to a stressed-out consultant attending a four-day conference at Haverford College in 1969.

Dismayed about the Vietnam War, Daniel Ellsberg (born 1931) had begun attending antiwar meetings. In August, he came to Haverford to attend the Thirteenth Triennial Conference of War Resisters International. Inspired by attendees' conviction that they could end the war—and their willingness to be imprisoned in the attempt—Ellsberg had a radical thought.

"As of this evening," he later wrote, "I realized that I had the power and the freedom to act the same way."

A month later, Ellsberg walked out of the RAND Corporation in Santa Monica, Calif., carrying the first of seven thousand pages of a secret report detailing the lies on which U.S. involvement in Vietnam was based. Newspapers would label the documents "The Pentagon Papers."

Born in Chicago, Ellsberg was the son of an engineer and a secretary. He graduated from Harvard in 1952 and then joined the Marine Corps, in which he commanded a rifle company. Ellsberg later earned a PhD in economics and joined RAND, a nonprofit think tank that advises the U.S. military. (RAND is short for **R**esearch **AN**d **D**evelopment.) His specialty was the control of nuclear weapons.

In 1964, Ellsberg joined the Pentagon to work on issues pertaining to Vietnam. The following year, he was transferred to Saigon to evaluate the situation in the countryside.

"It didn't take very long to discover in Vietnam that we weren't likely to be successful there," Ellsberg wrote in his 2002 book *Secrets*. "You don't have to be an ichthyologist to know when a fish stinks."

Ellsberg had been a committed cold warrior since high school. He remembered the Soviet Union's overthrow, in 1948, of a budding democracy in Czechoslovakia and the Berlin blockade. In Vietnam, he strongly desired a victory over that country's Soviet-backed communists. But then Ellsberg had seen documentation of Johnson administration lies that justified the Tonkin Gulf Resolution authorizing force in Vietnam. The chief result, he thought at the time, was to demonstrate Lyndon Johnson's toughness and assure his victory in that year's election.

In Vietnam, Ellsberg found a South Vietnamese army whose main criteria for promotion was connection to rich, Catholic, landowning families who supported the unelected president, Ngo Dinh Diem—an army that avoided the Viet Cong. In the Vung Tau province, Ellsberg and an officer were flagged down by a South Vietnamese lieutenant who explained that the road was closed because Viet Cong troops were crossing a mile or so ahead. The Americans ignored the officer's protests, drove on and saw nothing.

"He was worried that, if we went through, he wouldn't have any excuse for lying around," the officer explained. "He'd have to move out with his troops and find out if there really was anything in there."

Ellsberg observed a school-building program from which concrete was stolen and sold on the black market, usually going into private projects for the politically connected. The missing concrete was made up with sand, so new schools often began to crumble within a week. Such corruption, he concluded, made Vietnamese villagers angrier at their government and the Americans than if the work had never been done at all.

Ellsberg also witnessed the power of Vietnamese nationalism; he saw insurgents—boys—pop up in the middle of American battalions and fire at U.S. troops surrounding them. "They thought they were shooting at trespassers, foreign occupiers," he wrote, "that they had a right to be there and we didn't." And he noted much casual brutality when Americans and their allies burned houses and killed civilians for no compelling reason.

Finally, he observed the routine way in which U.S. officials lied. In 1967, on a long flight between Saigon and Washington, Ellsberg heard Secretary of Defense Robert McNamara despair about the deteriorating situation. Ten minutes after landing, McNamara told reporters, "Gentlemen, I've just come back from Vietnam, and I'm glad to be able to tell you that we're showing great progress in every dimension of our effort."

Already disillusioned, Ellsberg's despair deepened when he returned to a Pentagon in which everyone knowledgeable about the war knew it to be hopeless but said nothing. Asked to compile a study of the decision-making that had led to the conflict, he agreed to help draft one volume.

Ellsberg was a wonk. He didn't take on the project so much because he wanted to but rather to gain "access to the whole study for a comparative analysis and search for patterns." (His question: How could we have been so stupid?) What he eventually learned from the project was that Johnson's approach was not an anomaly. U.S. presidents had been lying about Vietnam for more than twenty years. Truman had aided the French secretly; Eisenhower had OK'd the crushing of political dissent; and Kennedy had sent the first troops and called them "advisers."

With no solution that might be called victory to allow U.S. withdrawal, Ellsberg placed his hopes on a new president. Those hopes died when it became apparent that Richard Nixon—equally reluctant to stain his reputation by losing a war—would escalate the war. Dismayed, Ellsberg turned to people he had previously dismissed: antiwar protesters.

"My knowledge of such people still came almost exclusively from media accounts, overwhelmingly negative, in which they were presented as being, in varying degree, extremist, simplistic, pro-Communist or pro-NLF, fanatic, anti-American, dogmatic," wrote Ellsberg, "I went to Haverford in part to find out if these labels were accurate."

Founded in 1921, War Resisters International and its U.S. affiliate, the War Resisters League, were full of such people. They had opposed both world wars, nuclear testing and civil defense drills. Many were involved in the civil rights movement.

Igal Roodenko (1917–1991), vice-chairman, had been arrested with Bayard Rustin in 1947 for violating a North Carolina law requiring segregated seating on buses. When the judge learned that Roodenko was Jewish, he sentenced him to ninety days—three times Rustin's sentence—as a lesson to other "Jews from New York" who might "upset the customs of the South."

Ralph DiGia (1914–2008), administrative secretary, was a conscientious objector jailed during World War II because the draft didn't recognize his secular rationale. In jail, he organized hunger strikes to integrate the dining halls.

In 1969, WRI—based in Manhattan—was focused on protest organizing. League minutes record two hundred participants in an April 4 vigil outside of New York's Selective Service headquarters and a "tremendous" turnout for a rally and parade the next day. Also on the agenda was a planned visit to Cuba and a campaign to organize tax resistance.

"Some felt that adults should match the challenge of the young who are saying 'no' to the draft by saying 'no' to war taxes," read the minutes.

It was a shoestring organization with a counterculture sensibility. WRL's April financial report showed "cash on hand" of $760 and payables of $14,385. In July, the group found it was no longer welcome at the New Jersey farm it had used for summer retreats. Too much marijuana and nude sunbathing, said the landlord.

Plus, the feds were watching. When WRL staged a fundraiser to finance relocation of its office, FBI agents recorded the names of those who entered. In May, after WRL offices were ransacked, New York police showed no inclination to investigate.

WRI had never convened in the United States. Some activists thought it shouldn't do so as long as the war continued. But others, arguing that the war made the United States the logical choice, carried the day. Haverford agreed to host the event for ten dollars per person, room and board. The theme, "Liberation and Revolution—Gandhi's Challenge," marked the centennial of Gandhi's birth and provided coherence to topics that ranged from U.S. militarism to economic justice in southern India.

There were last-minute changes. David Harris, married to folksinger Joan Baez, was scheduled to speak about draft resistance. But he had been jailed by the time the conference started.

Ellsberg was impressed by Robert Eaton (born 1944), a Quaker who in 1967 had sailed to Hanoi on the *Phoenix* to deliver medical supplies; in 1968, he had been arrested in Hungary for protesting Soviet occupation of Czechoslovakia. That week, he was scheduled to be imprisoned for refusing the draft. So, when attendees took a break on Wednesday to hold a vigil outside the U.S. courthouse where Eaton was being sentenced, Ellsberg went along.

Still professionally connected to RAND and the Pentagon, Ellsberg worried about being recognized. But he couldn't decline. "A man I admired was being sentenced to prison for an act of conscience," he recalled. "There was an invitation to join…in the company of one of the heroes of the century, Pastor Martin Niemöller, and others I admired no less. How could I not go?" Handing out leaflets left him feeling liberated. Niemöller (1892–1984), the anti-Nazi theologian most famous for his poem "First they came…," was a WRI vice-chair and conference participant.

Ellsberg's epiphany came the last day. In concluding remarks, Randy Kehler, head of WRL–San Francisco, told of being the only male left in his office. All of the others were in prison.

"When I go, it will be all women in the office," Kehler said. "But I can look forward to jail, without any remorse or fear…because I know that everyone here and lots of people around the world like you will carry on."

The audience stood and cheered. Ellsberg slipped into a men's room and sobbed.

"I had never cried like this before except when I learned that Bobby Kennedy was dead," he wrote. "A line kept repeating itself in my head: We are eating our young."

A few weeks later, Ellsberg asked a friend if he knew anyone with access to a copier.

A productive meeting, indeed.

1971
JOINING "ARNIE'S ARMY"

Veterans stick together. It's true of all sorts of veterans: '70s feminists, baby boomers, high school classmates and even former Enron employees.

Golfers do it, too. In 1971, Arnold Palmer—playing the U.S. Open at Merion Golf Club—noticed a shambling old man being ejected from the lobby. Palmer recognized John McDermott (1891–1971), who in 1911 had been the first American to win the U.S. Open. Tossing out such a man wouldn't do, decided Palmer, who shooed away club employees and escorted McDermott back inside.

"They talked golfer to golfer, champion to champion," wrote golf historian John Coyne, "and Palmer then arranged for McDermott to stay at the tournament as his special guest."

Born in Philadelphia, McDermott was the oldest child and only son of a mail carrier. He grew up on Fiftieth Street, only blocks from Aronimink Golf Club at Fifty-second Street and Chester Avenue. "J.J." McDermott began caddying at age nine. After his sophomore year at West Philadelphia High School, he dropped out to caddy full time.

McDermott was introduced to the game by Aronimink club professional Walter Reynolds, who had gotten his job when he was only nineteen. Golf was still new in Philadelphia—and, for that matter, in America—so there was room for youngsters.

In Europe, golf is very old. The word "golf" first appeared in 1457 when a statute was passed in Scotland to forbid it. The oldest course

At the 1971 U.S. Open, Arnold Palmer noticed employees shooing John McDermott, winner of the 1911 tournament, from the lobby of the Merion Cricket Club. Palmer intervened and made McDermott his guest for the day. *Lower Merion Historical Society.*

in the world is Edinburgh's Musselburgh Links where Mary, Queen of Scots, played in 1567. In America, golf officially arrived in 1873 when the Royal Montreal Club was formed. Fifteen years later, a Scotsman named John Reid built a three-hole course in Yonkers, New York, becoming the "father" of U.S. golf.

Golf came to Philadelphia in 1891. Harry C. Groome, an officer of the Philadelphia Country Club at Bala Cynwyd, was responsible for "suitable sports and pastimes" for members. But the club had just spent $40,000 on a polo field, so it didn't have a lot of spare cash.

"Golf appeared to us as a game very nearly related to croquet," said Groome years later. "We thought it might furnish mild amusement." He ordered a set of clubs and set three empty vegetable cans in the ground in a triangle measuring seventy-five yards on a side. But the clubs—available at twenty-five cents for thirty minutes—sat mostly unused.

In 1893, Philadelphians Marcellus Cox and Montgomery Wilcox encountered the game while summering in Canada. Excited, they hurried home to begin laying out a course near Devon. The club did not survive but perhaps prodded others to get serious. The Philadelphia Country Club laid out a nine-hole course in 1894, followed by the Philadelphia and Merion cricket clubs in 1895 and 1896.

By 1900, according to one estimate, 250,000 Americans played the game. Pennsylvania lagged behind New York and Massachusetts—with 165 and 157 courses, respectively—but the southeastern corner of the state was what one writer called a "beehive of bunkerland" with 17 clubs.

"Golf is a game which exactly suits Philadelphia and Philadelphians," observed Reid of Yonkers. "Neither boisterous nor effeminate, requiring alike consummate schooling and hard muscles and holding out almost boundless possibilities for fine playing and headwork, it naturally appeals to the people of that section."

But mostly *upper-class* people. Golf requires a lot of land, and the only people with enough were farmers—who had other uses for it—and the private clubs of the rich. According to historian G. William Domhoff, private clubs a century ago increasingly became tools with which America's upper class separated itself from both new immigrants and those who were homegrown but déclassé— déclassé like McDermott, whose father was Irish and recently arrived.

McDermott was small, scrawny and temperamental, "a loner," according to Philadelphia golf historian James W. Finegan. His privileges as a club employee gave him access to the course, but McDermott never had a member's easy manners. This would haunt him. He rarely drank, seldom dated and never married.

But golf was his life. In 1908, McDermott worked briefly at Merion's golf shop. Later, he taught briefly at the Camden County Country Club and then joined a Merchantville club as a professional. In 1911, he was hired by the Atlantic City Golf Club.

In style, McDermott mimicked the Scottish pros. He played with an "open" golf stance—body slouched and turned toward the target. Most consider this wrong because it can cause the ball to slice (curve away from the target), but it worked for McDermott. He also played the ball back of center and had a flat backswing that left the club wrapped around him rather than high. Again, both moves were mistakes for lesser golfers. But McDermott worked tirelessly on his game, rising before dawn to spend two or three hours hitting shots into an open newspaper, which served as his target.

"He would systematically move the paper back," wrote Finegan, "from 110 yards to 120 yards, then to 130, 140, 150 and so on as he went through his bag from niblick to mid-iron." One witness later told sports writer Red Smith that, after fifty or so balls, McDermott could collect them by simply folding up the four corners of his paper.

"What newspaper?" Smith supposedly asked.

"Oh," came the answer, "any tabloid would do."

At 8:00 a.m., he opened the club shop and proceeded to wait on members. At the end of the day, McDermott returned to the course and played until dark. Then, he putted by lamplight.

In 1910, only eighteen, McDermott won the Philadelphia Open and immediately aimed for the next level—the U.S. Open. First played in 1895, the U.S. Open for its first twenty-five years was an occasion for English and Scottish players to humiliate the Americans. But that year, McDermott—a journeyman golfer to most—surprised the field by battling into a three-way playoff with Alex Smith, a previous winner, and his brother. The Smiths were twice McDermott's age and vastly more experienced. McDermott lost, but he never played a bad round, scoring 75. And then?

According to Frost, "McDermott tracked Smith down afterward in the middle of his locker-room celebration, jammed a finger in his face and stunned everyone within earshot by warning the champ that he intended to beat him senseless next year." In the genteel world of early twentieth-century golf, this was terrible manners.

Yet he did win in 1911. McDermott started badly, scoring an 81 in the morning but redeeming himself with a 72 in the afternoon. That left him four strokes behind the leader, in a three-way tie for second. The leader had a bad second day, and the trio who had been contending for second found themselves battling for first. His opponents were less formidable than the Smiths, so McDermott carried the day.

Again, though, he gave the golfing community reason to frown. McDermott had gone into the match predicting his own victory. Gentlemen didn't do that. And he readily switched balls when a manufacturer offered $300 to the winner using its brand. It struck many as too grasping. Still, McDermott's win was historic, ending the domination of the British pros. He retained the title in 1912, but the McDermott streak was already running out.

McDermott failed to qualify for the 1912 British Open. After crowing that he would show the old country how golf was played, he shot a 93 and slunk out of Britain on a night ship. The British press roasted him. McDermott did better in 1913 but still didn't win.

Then, McDermott was widely condemned for his remark after beating British pros Harry Vardon and Ted Ray at a series of exhibition matches in the Poconos. Flushed with victory, the twenty-one-year-old stood on a chair and said, "We hope our foreign visitors had a good time, but we don't think they did, and we are sure they won't win the national [U.S.] Open."

Finegan called it "a display of arrogance that may have no equal in American golf." The USGA considered barring him from the Open. McDermott, initially unaware that he'd offended, apologized. Then, depressed, he finished eighth.

Investments went sour. In 1914, he missed a train and arrived at the British Open too late to play. Disappointed, he sailed for home on the *Kaiser Wilhelm II*, which collided with a grain ship in the English Channel. McDermott bobbed for hours in a lifeboat. At that year's U.S. Open, he finished at 300 ten strokes behind rising champion Walter Hagen. His familiar and abrasive self-confidence seemed missing.

A month later, McDermott blacked out in Atlantic City. A breakdown followed, and in 1916, his mother committed him to the Norristown State Hospital, from which he was never discharged, though he lived to almost eighty. According to Finegan, he was "usually seen lying on his bed—frequently he curls up in the fetal position." Paranoid, he claimed that everyone was against him, particularly golf officials who didn't want him to win. He scribbled for hours in notebooks. "There is little evidence," wrote Finnegan, "that any serious efforts were undertaken at Norristown to restore his mental health."

Fortunately, McDermott's sisters visited weekly and were allowed to take their Johnny on outings. Occasionally, they visited a golf course, where he watched but did not play.

Years later, on one such outing, McDermott entered the Merion club hoping to meet the players gathered for the 1971 U.S. Open. But he was dressed so poorly that he was ordered out. Appropriately, it was Palmer—the son of a golf course employee who, like McDermott, learned after hours—who brought him back. McDermott spent the day with the fans of "Arnie's Army," watching Lee Trevino (another player with hardscrabble origins) win an eighteen-hole playoff.

Two months later, he died in his sleep.

1972

GIVING FOOTBALL THE BOOT

A mericans love football. The rest of the world loves soccer. Without taking sides, let's consider the environment in which each sport thrives—or doesn't.

Haverford College has the oldest soccer program in the nation (founded 1895), and both its men's and women's teams frequently qualify for the National Collegiate Athletic Association (NCAA) playoffs. Football, however, died a natural death in 1972 after being handicapped for years by Haverford's high academic standards, commitment to equality and, possibly, a campus culture that—in the Vietnam era—was preternaturally conscious of its historic commitment to nonviolence.

Perhaps sociology professor William Hohenstein best expressed the thinking. A year after football died, he proposed strict terms to those proposing its revival. Filling the bench, he said, was not worth populating the campus with indifferent students or shortchanging Haverford's growing female population by devoting excessive resources to a male-only sport. "Football...cannot be allowed to get out of line with the budgets facing the other [athletic] programs," he told the *HBMC* (Haverford–Bryn Mawr College) *News*. "You cannot have the football team stopping on the trip home for steak dinners while the cross country team is given a dollar a man to eat at Gino's."

Football began at Haverford in 1879, just a few years after the 1873 agreement on intercollegiate rules by Columbia, Rutgers, Princeton and Yale that arguably launched college-level play. Earlier versions of the game were played at American colleges as early as the 1820s.

Soccer powerhouse Haverford College once had a football team, too. But football died a natural death in 1972 after the college refused to cut corners and compromise principles to help it thrive. *Haverford College.*

Nationally, college football's popularity grew rapidly and then exploded in the economic boom of the Roaring Twenties. Celebrity coaches like Knute Rockne began making product endorsements. Pro teams emerged, and scandals involving recruitment and subsidies for student athletes soon followed. In the 1930s, limited subsidies to college players were permitted, paving the way for the free ride many players receive today.

There was resistance. Harvard president Charles Eliot deplored the "unwholesome desire for victory" that affected many athletes and coaches. He wanted football banned. As recently as 1966, Reverend Theodore M. Hesburgh, then president of Notre Dame, refused the football team permission to play a postseason bowl game that might interfere with preparations for finals.

But according to historian Allen Sack, most presidents and boards of trustees collaborated willingly. "Starved for students and financial support," wrote Sack in the *Chronicle of Higher Education* in 2001, "presidents in the late 19th and early 20th centuries needed a bridge to connect the high culture of academe with the external constituencies upon which institutions depend for survival." Meanwhile, many of the business types who dominated college boards thought that sport—with its teamwork, discipline and no-nonsense problem solving—was a useful counter to the classroom's "wasteful intellectual theorizing."

As a result, the phrase "student athlete" produces snickers on many campuses. But not at Haverford. The college has never offered athletic scholarships or had separate admission standards for athletes. All students must meet the same standards, and athletic success has nothing to do with whether one remains on campus. Those who play for Haverford do so only because they find it fun.

That's how Haverford thinks sports should be, said athletic director Greg Kannerstein (1941–2009). Believing that athletics produces well-rounded individuals, the college considers it more important to provide every student that experience than to produce stars or win championships.

"Our guiding philosophy is to make it possible for students to give 100 percent to their teams and still never slight academics," wrote Kannerstein in a 2006 letter to prospective students and parents. Yet Haverford defines "100 percent" differently: coaches limit practice to two hours per day, not three to four hours as is common at many large schools; faculty, in return, don't teach at prime practice and game hours.

A 1972 manual for new students described the athletic program as "relaxed."

"The 'blood and guts' attitude just isn't around," the freshmen were informed. "Neither is there much of the strict discipline that high school and college teams often have to endure. Haverfordians usually take up a sport for exercise, personal satisfaction and fun, not just to win. In fact, some Haverford teams have almost given up winning altogether."

Exhibit A: the football team. According to Kannerstein, the team performed well in the 1950s. But rule changes in the 1960s established the two-platoon system and the right of coaches to substitute players at will. What that meant was that teams could have twice as many players on the bench as the eleven required on the field.

"Two-platoon" is actually a euphemism. Many schools have fifty or more players—enough to field four full teams with change left over. Some have as many as a hundred players.

"Most squads in the 1950s had twenty to thirty players," said Kannerstein, who was an assistant baseball coach in the early '70s. But when opposing teams ballooned, Haverford couldn't match their size. So, as Haverford players tired over the course of a game, its opponents—by sending in substitutes—always remained fresh.

"They would wear us down and chase us off the field in the second half," said Kannerstein. From 1959 through 1971, the Haverford football team never won more than one or two games per year. That dampened enthusiasm. Player Joe Quinlan, '75, would later lament that the sport died of indifference.

"It was tough for fans to root for teams that they knew were going to lose," said Quinlan in a 1972 column in the *HBMC News*. "It was tough for the players because they would hear the comments and see the look of defeat and sometimes contempt on people's faces."

Some of that contempt was for the sport itself. It was the '70s. Nixon was on the throne, Vietnam was grinding on and, in many minds, football summarized the issues of the day.

"To right-wing political leaders," wrote sports historian Benjamin Rader, "football was a miniature school for testing and nurturing physical and moral vigor." Proponents of the counterculture, however, believed that "only a nation addicted to the violence of a sport like football…could pursue such an immoral and brutal war."

Nixon was known to love football. During the 1971 NFL season, he phoned coaches George Allen of the Washington Redskins and Don Shula of the Miami Dolphins to offer advice.

But Haverford College was not Nixon territory. As the 1972 election loomed, a fall campus poll showed that 81 percent of students favoring the candidacy of Democratic nominee (and tennis lover) George McGovern. Only 8 of the remaining 19 percent favored Nixon; another 8 percent was undecided, and 3 percent favored minor parties. Before the academic year had ended, the *HBMC News* would respond to the emerging Watergate scandal with an early call for Nixon's resignation.

The players, too, sensed that football was not cool. When the season was scrubbed, junior Mike Ferrell, '74, complained of what he perceived as Haverford's increasing elitism. Was it a coincidence, he asked the *HBMC News*, that the freshman class had produced only six African Americans—a decrease—and only five football players? Player Bill Willis, '75, protested a sports columnist's characterization of football as a "working class" game. "At this pseudo-pacifistic school, there seems to be a strong aversion to playing organized football," he wrote. "As one of these working class jocks, I strongly resent the…condescending tone."

Ironically, the 1971 season hadn't been all that bad. Haverford had whomped Scranton University 51–13 in a game in which, said the *HBMC News*, it "dominated the opposition in every respect." Senior David Parham, '72, connected on fourteen of nineteen passes to gain 196 yards and three touchdowns. This was followed by a satisfying 22–21 win over rival Swarthmore.

In the fall of 1972, however, just twenty-one players turned up at the fall training camp. Fifty-four, meanwhile, went out for soccer that year. Head coach Dana Swan had expected twenty-nine, but eight dropped out over the summer—five for unhealed injuries. Of the rest, five were freshman and one, George Shotzbarger, had never played football before. Parham and another Haverford star, Doug Nichols, '92, had graduated. At this point, Swan said later, "winning or losing became secondary…it became a simple matter of survival."

Then came the Cheyney scrimmage. The small squad worked hard daily, but Swan was blunt: with so few players, things did not look good. He offered no commitment that the team would even begin the season. Team members responded by recruiting a couple of extra players.

What Swan needed, he later told the *HBMC News*, was a game situation to fairly assess the team's prospects. So, on September 9, it played a nonleague scrimmage with Cheyney State, a larger school with more players and a different philosophy about sports.

"We had thirteen able-bodied survivors," recalled Kannerstein.

It was a big story for a few days. The *New York Times* and *Philadelphia Bulletin*—which reported Haverford games in two-inch stories, if at all— spent nine and twenty-five inches, respectively, explaining the team's demise. The *Cleveland Plain Dealer* used the Haverford story in an editorial lamenting the professionalization of college sports. Local sports writers asked a few tough questions of schools with subsidized programs and then moved on to other subjects.

The following year, when a task force of students and faculty tried to gin up enthusiasm for the sport's return, Swan insisted that he would need forty to forty-five players for a credible program. And that was the end of that. Even the alumni didn't grumble too loudly. Today, it seems perfectly normal to celebrate Homecoming with a soccer game on Walton Field where, long ago, football was played.

"The only time football really comes up is when other schools' administrators ask how we managed to get rid of it," said Kannerstein. "I think they're envious."

Lenny's Monument

Few people get to erect their own monuments. But no one could have a more appropriate memorial than Phillies outfielder Lenny Dykstra, whose career and Main Line residency were perfectly summarized by the tread marks and banged-up tree he left on Darby-Paoli Road in 1991.

Dykstra (born 1963) spun out his new red Mercedes after leaving Smokey Joe's tavern in Wayne with teammate Darren Daulton and a blood-alcohol content of 0.178 (the legal limit was 0.10). He played ball the same way.

"Lenny Dykstra…was a man with no speed limits," ESPN sports reporter Jayson Stark later said. "All his accelerator pedals hit the floor. That's the way he played. That's the way he drove. That's the way he lived. He was his own little amusement-park attraction—Mr. Dude's Wild Ride."

Dykstra's style was also responsible for injuries that ended Dykstra's major league career after a mere twelve seasons.

Dykstra started out in the minors and rose to prominence with the 1986 New York Mets before being traded to the Phillies in 1989. In the '86 league playoffs, Dykstra hit a home run against the Houston Astros that brought the Mets a 6–5 victory. The team's subsequent World Series victory over the Boston Red Sox further lifted Dykstra's profile. He'd been with the team only a year.

But what a team it was! Pitcher Dwight Gooden based a reputation on his ninety-seven-mile-per-hour fastball. Hitter Darryl Strawberry remains the Mets' all-time leader in home runs and runs batted in. William "Mookie" Wilson, a switch-hitter known for speed, was inducted into the

Phillies outfielder Lenny Dykstra, according to one sports reporter, was "a man with no speed limits." This explains his repeated injuries, his short career and the 1991 spinout at this curve that carried his red Mercedes into a tree (right). *Mark E. Dixon.*

Mets' Hall of Fame in 1995. With Bobby Ojeda, Gary Carter and Keith Hernandez, the '86 team had powerful hitting, acrobatic defense and white-hot pitching.

Dykstra's teammates admired his fielding and speed. The fans liked his flashy and determined catching. "Fence, no fence, it didn't matter," said one observer. "He was catching the ball." Even his dirty uniform—a result of sliding into stolen bases—amused the crowds. Dubbed one of the "Partners in Grime" with second baseman Wally Backman, Dykstra got one of his first endorsements from the company that made his uniform. "They liked me because mine was always dirty, and they could show how their product stood up," he said.

In many ways, he was just a larger version of the kid who grew up playing Little League baseball in Southern California. He had also played football and once got a concussion when he tried hockey. But Dykstra lived for baseball. "I used to take Ping-Pong balls and roll them around on my bed," he later recalled. "I thought it would help me follow a pitch and help me pick up the rotation of the ball."

Dykstra even avoided reading because he didn't want to hurt his eyes. "Wanted to keep them strong for baseball," he said.

His first attempt to enter the big leagues was in the late 1970s, when a teenaged Dykstra and several friends scaled the fence at Anaheim Stadium one December 25. They wanted the experience of playing on a professional field and thought that security would be slack on Christmas.

"We had our gloves and bats and we must have had 70 balls with us," said Dykstra. "We were hitting flies and taking BP [batting practice]."

A police helicopter fluttered over. Via a loudspeaker, the boys were told to drop their equipment, stand in centerfield and wait for the copter to land. Instead, they scattered and Dykstra got away. "S--t, we weren't robbing a bank or kidnapping babies," he said.

Critics thought that Dykstra never picked up on the subtleties of baseball. "He had no restraint in playing the game," said baseball historian John Shiffert. "You just can't play baseball with a football mentality: 'Arrrghh! Let's run through a wall and go kill 'em.' Do that, and you'll get hurt. He did." Dykstra, for example, habitually hit for the fences, an unnecessary habit that could, and did, injure his back.

Initially, though, he fit right in with the rowdy '86 Mets, perhaps the last major league team to completely ignore corporate sensitivities about players' partying.

After home games, the Mets gathered at a blue-collar tavern called Finn MacCool's, where they drank with the fans, bought rounds and were often seen in the early morning carrying teammates home, trailed by giggling female groupies. The Mets kept a beer-stocked refrigerator in the locker room at Shea Stadium. On mornings after home games, trainers often arrived to find men passed out on the floor.

Moralists clucked when players smoked in the dugout. Dykstra, famous for his wad of chewing tobacco, was blamed for encouraging kids to use the stuff. He later made a TV ad to atone: "Copy my hustle. Copy my desire," he urged. "But, please, don't copy my tobacco use."

It didn't stop there. Both Gooden and Strawberry were suspended for cocaine use during their careers. Strawberry is divorced from two wives, both of whom accused him of assault, and served time on drug charges. Ojeda was the lone survivor of a 1993 boating accident during spring training that killed fellow pitchers Steve Olin and Tim Crews. Dykstra was repeatedly accused of using steroids during his career.

"We were throwbacks," said Ojeda. "We were like, 'Gimme a steak, gimme a f--kin' beer, gimme a smoke and get the f--k out of our way.'"

Management looked the other way. After celebrating players did thousands of dollars of damage to the plane carrying them home from a league championship game, manager David Johnson chewed them out but only briefly. "You know what I think?" he said. "I think in the next four games, you'll put enough money in these guys' pockets to cover this. So f--- this bulls--t."

Opponents—especially other teams' fans—thought that the Mets were "a bunch of a--holes." In the '86 season alone, the Mets were involved in four bench-clearing fights, which only seemed to rev them up. "You love to win a game after a fight," said Dykstra after beating the Cincinnati Reds individually and as a group. The team then rubbed it in with a (double platinum) rap, "Get Metsmerized," in which Dykstra collaborated with Strawberry, Gooden, Rafael Santana and others:

> *With control and power of a diesel train*
> *throwin' tombstone bullets and a ball 'n' chain.*
> *Lenny D., your spirit's contagious*
> *what ya do to your body is really outrageous.*
> *Team's real hot, stand up proud*
> *Do the wave, shout it loud!*
> *Get Metsmerized, Get Metsmerized.*

And yet, the Mets still finished the '86 season 108-54, the best record in baseball and twenty games ahead of the next National League East team.

The following year, Dykstra's $92,500 salary was more than doubled—to $202,500.

Dykstra continued to produce for the Mets in 1987 and '88 but struck out more than he walked. Traded to the Phillies, the newly married Dykstra got another pay boost—to $700,000—and bought a house in Devon.

It was an unusual address, said Shiffert. Since the closing of Connie Mack Stadium in 1970, most athletes have lived in South Jersey, near the sports complex. Perhaps Terri Dykstra was trying to settle him down. Whatever the reason, he now had to drive to parties.

On May 5, 1991, Dykstra and about a half-dozen other players gathered at the home of teammate John Kruk, who was being married the next day. The gathering turned into an impromptu bachelor party and eventually moved to Smokey Joe's. When the players started drifting away after midnight, Dykstra offered Daulton a ride home to Jersey. The Blue Route (I-476) had not yet been opened, so the two men headed south from Lancaster Avenue through residential Wayne, past the Willows and south on Darby-Paoli Road toward Route 320. Neither wore a seat belt.

The last thing Daulton remembered was the passenger side of the car skidding toward some trees. The only trees at the crash site—just south of Saw Mill Road—are on the driver's side. Dykstra—doing about fifty in a thirty-five-mile-per-hour zone—apparently lost control rounding a bend and put the car in a spin. Daulton suffered a fractured left eye socket.

Dykstra, who was found in the back seat, had a broken collarbone, broken ribs, a slightly punctured lung and a broken bone beneath his right eye. Cited for drunk driving, Dykstra pleaded no contest and, as community service, created a video, "Cruisin' not Boozin'," that Bryn Mawr Rehab used to discourage teens from drunk driving.

Four days after the wreck, Dykstra left Bryn Mawr Hospital sounding like a public service announcement: "What happened was...something that maybe, ah, from here on out, hopefully it can have a positive effect on the people who watch me play," he told reporters. "You can't drink and drive."

Hospital workers, however, painted a different picture. Anonymous ER employees told news reporters that Dykstra had arrived cursing, spitting and punching. "I don't know what he remembers," said one. "I have no idea what was drug- and pain-induced. He was not a gentleman."

Later, Dykstra became so polite and considerate—giving away CDs to members of the staff—that opinions mellowed.

Dykstra was disabled for sixty days and so received only a $100,000 raise—to $2.3 million—the following year. But he came back strong in 1992 and especially '93, when he hit a three-run homer against Toronto in the sixth game of the World Series, which the Phillies nevertheless lost 8–6. In 1995, Dykstra signed a four-year $25 million contract.

But the injuries continued. Three months after the wreck, Dykstra refractured his collarbone bouncing off an unpadded fence at the Cincinnati Reds' Riverfront Stadium. Manager Jim Fregosi said it was the fence's fault.

Back injuries followed, and Dykstra retired at the end of the 1996 season, when he was only thirty-three.

In the following decade, Dykstra launched a string of high-end car washes under his own name, a jet charter company and *Player's Club*, a magazine for pro athletes. In 2009, however, Dykstra—whose net worth was estimated at $58 million the previous year—filed for bankruptcy. He told a CNBC reporter that he had been sleeping in his car and hotel lobbies.

All that, eloquently illustrated by one scarred tree.

BIBLIOGRAPHY

Anonymous. *The Mirrors of Washington.* New York: G.P. Putnam's Sons, 1921.

Carter, Alice A. *The Red Rose Girls: An Uncommon Story of Art and Love.* New York: Harry N. Abrams, 2002.

DeGraw, Ronald. *The Red Arrow: A History of One of the Most Successful Suburban Transit Companies in the World.* Haverford, PA: Haverford Press, 1972.

Domhoff, G. William. *Who Rules America Now?* Boston, MA: Waveland Press, 1997.

Dykstra, Lenny. *Nails: The Inside Story of an Amazin' Season.* Garden City, NY: Doubleday & Company, 1987.

Ellsberg, Daniel. *Secrets: A Memoir of Vietnam and the Pentagon Papers.* New York: Viking, 2003.

Faderman, Lillian. *Surpassing the Love of Men: Romantic Friendship and Love Between Women from the Renaissance to the Present.* New York: HarperCollins Publishers, 1998.

Finegan, James W. *A Centennial Tribute to Golf in Philadelphia: The Champions and the Championships, the Clubs and the Courses.* Philadelphia, PA: Golf Association of Philadelphia, 1996.

Halberstam, David. *The Coldest Winter: America and the Korean War.* New York: Hyperion, 2007.

Heller, Rita R. "The Women of Summer: The Bryn Mawr Summer School for Women Workers, 1921–1938." PhD thesis, Rutgers University, 1986.

Howe, Neil, and William Strauss. *Generations: The History of America's Future, 1584 to 2069.* New York: Harpers, 1991.

Hoyt, Edwin P. *The Goulds: A Social History.* New York: Weybreidge and Talley, 1969.

Jensen, Mike. "Daulton Discusses the Accident." *Philadelphia Inquirer*, May 11, 1991.

3M.. "For Some on Hospital Staff, Life with Lenny Wasn't Easy." *Philadelphia Inquirer*, May 14, 1991.

Kirkpatrick, Sidney. *The Revenge of Thomas Eakins.* New Haven, Connecticut and London: Yale University Press, 2006.

Marshall, Logan. *The Sinking of the Titanic.* Bellevue, WA: Seattle Miracle Press, 1997.

McFeely, William S. *Portrait: The Life of Thomas Eakins.* New York and London: Norton, 2007.

Michener, James. "Philadelphia's Main Line: Suburbia at its Best." *Holiday* magazine (April 1953).

Olson, Stanley. *Elinor Wylie: A Biography.* New York: Dial Press, 1979.

Rubinstein, William D. *The Myth of Rescue: Why the Democracies Could Not Have Saved More Jews from the Nazis.* New York: Routledge, 1999.

Schlenther, Boyd Stanley. "The English Is Swallowing Up Their Language: Welsh Ethnic Ambivalence in Colonial Pennsylvania and the Experience of David Evans." *Pennsylvania Magazine of History & Biography* 114: 201–228. Historical Society of Pennsylvania.

Temple University Urban Archives. Annual Report Collection. *Lincoln Institution and Educational Home*, 1869–72, 1874–77, 1882, 1885, 1887, 1891, 1908–10, 1912–20.

"War Resisters League Records." Unpublished manuscripts. Swarthmore Peace Archive, Swarthmore College, 1923–98.

Wills, Garry. *Negro President: Jefferson and the Slave Power.* New York: Houghton Mifflin Harcourt, 2003.

ABOUT THE AUTHOR

Mark E. Dixon is a writer in Wayne who has written a local history column for *Main Line Today* magazine since 2003. He began his journalism career in 1977, writing for newspapers in the Midwest and the South and then for trade publications in Dallas. A native of East Grand Rapids, Michigan, Dixon moved in 1987 to the Philadelphia area, where he worked in public relations for five years and subsequently as a freelance writer.

Visit us at
www.historypress.net